A BLACK HAWK WAR GUIDE

Landmarks, Battlefields, Museums & Firsthand Accounts

BEN STRAND

Foreword by Kealan Hamilton-Youngbird

THE
History
PRESS

Published by The History Press
Charleston, SC
www.historypress.com

Front cover images: *Múk-a-tah-mish-o-káh-kaik, Black Hawk, Prominent Sac Chief*, George Catlin, 1832, oil on canvas. *Smithsonian American Art Museum, Gift of Mrs. Joseph Harrison Jr., 1985.66.2.* "When I painted this chief, he was dressed in a plain suit of buckskin, with strings of wampum in his ears and on his neck, and held in his hand, his medicine-bag, which was the skin of a black hawk, from which he had taken his name, and the tail of which made him a fan, which he was almost constantly using." From Catlin's *Letters and Notes*, vol. 2, no. 56, 1841; *Indian Campaign of 1832: Map of the Country*, by Colonel Edwin Rose, 1832. *Courtesy of the Map Library at the University of Illinois at Urbana–Champaign.*

Back cover images: Abraham Lincoln bronze bust. *University of Wisconsin–Whitewater. Photo by Ben Strand*; entrance to the city of Fort Atkinson, Fort Atkinson, Wisconsin. *Photo by Leo Strand*; Milton House. Milton, Wisconsin. *Photo by Leo Strand.*

All images courtesy of Ben Strand unless otherwise noted.

First published 2021

ISBN 9781467146098

Library of Congress Control Number: 2020945750

Notice: The information in this book is true and complete to the best of our knowledge. It is offered without guarantee on the part of the author or The History Press. The author and The History Press disclaim all liability in connection with the use of this book.

CONTENTS

CONTENTS

FOREWORD

The Forceful Displacement of the Sauk and Fox Tribes from the Great Lakes to Indian Territory

My Sauk name is Sékito, which translates as "The Thunder that Scares You." My English name is Kealan Hamilton-Youngbird. I am a registered member of the Sac and Fox Nation of Oklahoma. The U.S. government used multiple treaties that were forced, unjust compromises and created conflicts to ensure the spread of European settlers into the West, forcing my people onto unsettled lands west of the Mississippi.

At the time of European contact, my people lived near Saginaw Bay of Lake Huron and Green Bay of Lake Michigan. The Sauk tribe built the large village of Saukenuk in Rock Island, Illinois. The Fox tribe built smaller villages along the western shore of the Mississippi River. The Sauk and Fox tribes were originally two separate tribes during the 1700s. A French attack on the Fox tribe caused the two tribes to band together. The U.S. government merged the Sauk and Fox tribes as one beginning with the Treaty of St. Louis in 1804. This treaty was the first of many that would push my people from their homelands in Rock Island. There was no compromise. My people were tricked and manipulated into ceding away all of our land east of the Mississippi. This treaty was protested by my people due to the fact that the signatories did not have authority to make any agreements on our behalf. The Treaty of 1804 stated that the Sauk and Fox could remain on the land as long as they kept peace with the settlers. This, too, was a promise that was not kept and amended in other treaties that followed.

Between the years 1828 and 1831, the Sauk and Fox were forced to share land with the settlers, who continued to move into our villages. The settlers demanded that my people should be removed from our village. Can you imagine that? Your people have lived on these lands and in their lodges for more than a century and people from a foreign country who have invaded your home demand that you leave everything you have ever known—everything you worked for. Our ancestors were buried on these lands. It is sacred to us. It is a part of our culture to take care of the graves and keep a connection to our history. This didn't sit well with our war leader, Black Hawk. He refused to leave. Our people and the settlers lived side by side for some time. This didn't go well. Problems continued to grow as settlers pushed more and more of our people from their lands and lodges.

On May 28, 1830, President Andrew Jackson was empowered by the Indian Removal Act to send commissioners to negotiate removal treaties. What is the Indian Removal Act, you ask? It was a bill advocated by President Jackson, who believed that any eastern tribe members who wanted to remain a part of their tribe and practice their culture should move west of the Mississippi.

By 1831, the governor of Illinois, backed by the Indian Removal Act, was demanding that U.S. authorities remove Black Hawk and our people from our village of Saukenuk to Iowa. The ordered attack lead by General Gaines pushed my people to the western side of the Mississippi River. Then came the Corn Treaty of 1831. General Gaines called a meeting at Rock River to forge a new treaty that would require that we could not return to the eastern side of the Mississippi without government permission. It also allowed for roads and forts to be built on Sauk and Fox territory. If we agreed, we were promised to be supplied with enough food and corn that would equal what we were to leave behind. This did not happen. We were removed to western banks of the Mississippi River (present-day Iowa).

After the U.S. government had left my people displaced and starving, Black Hawk began a campaign to return to our homelands and our village of Saukenuk. Black Hawk—followed by some of our men, women, children and elders—tried to return to Rock Island to reclaim the crops we left behind. To the authorities, this was seen as an act of war and began what would later be known as the "Black Hawk War" of 1832. A militia was sent to hunt us down. Even though our return to Saukenuk wasn't an act of war, Black Hawk and our people had to flee. Black Hawk later sent some of our men with a white flag of peace, but they were fired upon, and one of them was killed. The hunt for Black Hawk and his followers went on for fifteen weeks. On August 2, 1832, my people were massacred at what was labeled as the Battle at Bad Axe. Black Hawk and the remaining survivors surrendered. Black Hawk, our respected war leader, was imprisoned.

With Black Hawk out of the way, the U.S. government leaned heavily on the cooperation of the Fox chief Keyokuk to persuade the Sauk and Fox people to relocate to Iowa. He signed treaties in 1836, 1837 and 1842 that ceded away a total of 12 million acres of our lands in Iowa to the United States. In the treaty of 1842, Keyokuk agreed to move our people to a reservation in present-day Kansas. Keyokuk and the Sauk and Fox departed Iowa for Kansas in 1845.

By the spring of 1846, we were trying to adjust to life on the headwaters of the Osage River. The land and territory proved extremely challenging in our pursuit of the way of life we had lived for generations. Many of the Fox people left Iowa under protest. They had no interest in adapting to life on the plains. In the winter of 1851, an estimated one hundred of our people (mainly of the Fox tribe) returned to Iowa. In 1856, the State of Iowa enacted a law allowing the Foxes to reside in the state. In 1857, the Sauk and Fox of Iowa purchased eighty acres in Tama County, Iowa. More of our people were to follow them to their return to Iowa. For the remaining tribal members, more settlers moving into the Kansas reservation meant yet another treaty negotiation to remove the Sauk and Fox into Indian Territory.

On February 18, 1867, five of our chiefs affixed their mark to the treaty that would cede away any of our land in Kansas and remove all remaining tribal members to the Indian Territory. One of our chiefs, Mokohoko, was not there to sign this treaty. Almost two years passed before our people were removed from Kansas. The trip from Kansas to Indian Territory took nineteen days. Mokohoko and more than two hundred of his followers stayed behind. He was not in favor of being removed once again, and in 1875, he secured permission for the band to remain in Kansas.

By the time my people arrived in Indian Territory, the years that passed from the time of European contact to our removal to Oklahoma, the Sauk and Fox people that once thrived and numbered in the thousands were close to dissipated. Our language, our dances, our feasts, our ceremonies, our culture, our way of life—these were all viewed as barriers to "Indian progress." We were being acculturated, and in hopes to avoid erasing all signs of our history, we were forced to go along with all of it.

But through any uncertainty and adversity, my people are still here. We have managed to hold on to our traditional ways. We still feast and have ceremonies. We still know our history. We still dance.

Kealan Hamilton-Youngbird. *Mark E. Lawson.*

FOREWORD

The U.S. government used multiple treaties, little compromise and much conflict to ensure the spread of European settlers into the West, pushing my people onto unsettled lands west of the Mississippi and ultimately splitting my people into three separate bands: Meskwaki (the Sac and Fox Tribe of the Mississippi in Iowa), Ne ma ha ha ki (the Sac and Fox Nation of Missouri in Kansas and Nebraska) and Sa ki wa ki (the Sac and Fox Nation of Oklahoma).

My name is Sékito. I am a descendant of survivors. I have been assimilated, but I am not defeated. I will carry on my way of life in the two worlds I currently reside in. To tell *my* story is to share the stories of all the indigenous people of this continent. We are living, breathing history. WE ARE STILL HERE!

Thank you.

KEALAN HAMILTON-YOUNGBIRD

PREFACE

Abe Lincoln passed this way and had his horse stolen. Honest Abe was right here, in 1832, serving as a soldier in the Black Hawk War. At this spot he was honorably discharged from the U.S. militia. Since he had no horse, he walked back to his home in Illinois with George Harrison.

George Harrison the Beatle? Abe Lincoln in Wisconsin? Honest Abe, a soldier?

The battered sign outside a Wisconsin tavern seemed to be a prank posted by locals tired of Illinois tourists. When you are traveling through the state that birthed the satirical newspaper *The Onion*, one can never be too careful. But the faded wooden sign outside of Cold Spring, Wisconsin, was accurate. Close to two hundred years ago, America's most examined and lauded president, Abraham Lincoln, had been a young militia member engaged against a group of Sauk and Fox and unaffiliated tribal members. Abraham Lincoln evokes many images in the minds of American, but frontier soldier is not one of them.

I was born in and grew up in Dodgeville, Wisconsin, the small town named after Henry Dodge, the state's first governor, a slave owner and a central figure in the Black Hawk War of 1832. The stories of Native Americans in Wisconsin were not shared during my primary education. While copies of the Frontier Dan series and works by Louis L'Amour were widely popular in the public library, any mention of Native Americans or frontier living were relegated to the far far West—the West of Wyoming, Nevada and New

Mexico, rather than the 1820s Northwest Territory of Iowa, Michigan, Wisconsin and Illinois. The more seedy details of Henry Dodge's role as a slaveholder and land squatter weren't widely shared in the public elementary curriculum in the 1980s. Henry Dodge is remembered more as a genial frontiersman, not a bullying slave owner who led the regional effort to impose President Jackson's American Indian removal policy of 1830.

The two largest swimming holes near Dodgeville are the Black Hawk Recreational Area in Highland (established on July 4, 1972) and the Governor Dodge State Park (named in honor of Dodge in 1955), a few miles north of Dodgeville. These dueling parks advertised the recreational benefits of the man-made lakes created by impounding small creeks. The lakes provide a refuge for tourists to fish and swim in and were named after two of the preeminent figures of the early 1800s in the Northwest Territory. I spent a fair number of days at each of these parks while growing up, but the significance of their namesakes and the cultural history each represented didn't occur to me. While I grew up in the middle of the Old Northwest Territory, I was a stranger to its history.

For generations, the legacy of Native Americans in the Midwest was politely omitted. When I asked one old-timer at a small-town museum about the First Nations that had been in the area, he confessed that they were all "Out West" and that this area was pretty well clear of any civilization when Americans and Europeans began arriving. Another historic site volunteer strenuously noted that none of the massacres of the Black Hawk War occurred in their county. By the time settlers arrived, she assured me, there were only old paths and Indian arrowheads left.

Today, the stories, cultures and legacy of the numerous communities that lived in the Midwest for thousands of years before European immigrants arrived are slowly becoming more discoverable. Small business owners who had named their products or companies after the Kickapoos or Winnebagos have decided to alter their branding to be more conscious of cultural appropriation. Universities and K–12 educators are working closer with First Nation communities to ensure that their history is part of the narrative taught in the classroom.

This guide provides a local's insight and tips in accessing sites researched and preserved in the old Northwest Territory. It builds on the work of generations of historians and archivists and, when possible, highlights the inspiration and strength the First Nations spread—and still advocate for.

ACKNOWLEDGEMENTS

This guide provides a local's insight and tips in accessing sites researched and preserved by academic histories, dedicated historical societies and the collections of the Black Hawk papers at the Illinois Historical Society, the Smithsonian, the Hathi Trust and other physical and digital libraries, as well as, of course, the First Nations of the Meskwakis and Asakiwakis.

Especially helpful in sparking my interest in this project was the unmatched historical work by Cecil D. Eby, *That Disgraceful Affair*. Other works have also documented the route of the Black Hawk War, including *Along the Black Hawk Trail* by William Stark in 1984, William Thomas Hagan's *Report on Black Hawk's Route through Wisconsin in 1949* and *The Life and Adventures of Black Hawk with Sketches of Keokuk, the Sauk and Fox Indians, and the Late Black Hawk War* by Benjamin Drake published in 1849.

The patience and guidance from Juaquin Hamilton and Kealan Hamilton-Youngbird provided the proper foundation and heart for this book.

Encouragement, both explicit and implicit, was provided by Steve Hannah, who gave voice to the Midwest's hidden stories, and Richard Haas, who captured and shared Black Hawk's countenance in his larger-than-life mural. Thanks also to Betty Schoonover, Ed Van Gemert, Deb Holt, Richard Panek, Ben Logan, Edna Meudt, Nancy Johnson, Bob Karrow, Maud Casey, Harlan McKosato, Lauren Mayer, Michael J. Mayosky, Julie Nelson, Dan Richardson, Richard Sorenson, Erin Beasley, Jeanette Russell, Bob Arnold, Doug Welch, Ryan LeCloux, Erik Flesch, Mary Antoine, Jennifer Tigges, Chris Boyd, Mark E. Lawson, Ryan Finn and Ben Gibson.

Acknowledgements

This effort was enriched by the dedication of Iowa, Illinois and Wisconsin's tourism leaders and local historical societies that work every day to spread the joy of travel.

The resources and advice from the staff and volunteers at numerous local museums and historic sites provided key assistance in making the guide accessible. Thank you to the Milton House Museum, the Hoard Museum, the Hauberg Museum Black Hawk State Historic Site and the estate of Lorine Niedecker.

This work is dedicated to my eighth-grade social studies teacher, Dan Schwarz, who assigned his students to research the origin of a town in Wisconsin and write about it in an insurmountable one-page paper—my choice was New Diggings, Wisconsin.

Thanks also to the online and in-person assistance from the following libraries: UW–Platteville, UW–Whitewater, UW–Madison's Memorial Library, the Hathi Trust, Newberry Library, the Research Center at the Oklahoma Historical Society and the Wisconsin Historical Society Library and Archives. Much gratitude and thanks goes to the extra microfiche reproduction services of the University of Illinois and the Smithsonian American Art Museum and its curation, preservation and digital access of its collections.

Many thanks to Sadie, Leo and Kari for traipsing through history on many weekends.

INTRODUCTION

T he harried course that Black Hawk and his followers traversed in the summer of 1832 was not an established path that could be cemented in time like the Freedom Trail in Boston, which courses through the city pavement emblazoned with a wide red line painted down the middle of the sidewalk to help tourists view sites of interest. There is no Black Hawk trail proper, as there was never an established path, road or wilderness trail that could be traveled by following freshly painted guideposts. While parts of the path that Black Hawk led his people on did at times follow traditional Native American trails, much of the route was a haphazard retreat by elders, families, children and warriors. This trail of necessity was traversed by an entire community that was desperate to not be found. How does a mass of humanity, estimated at nearly 1,200 souls, hide itself from a pursuing militia?

Questions about the exact location of Black Hawk's route—traveled by a group named the "British Band" for their prior allegiance to the British— have been researched and debated by historians since the conclusion of the hostilities. A good deal of the confusion can be attributed to the inhospitable terrain that the Sauk and Fox tribes utilized to confound the American military forces. Known as the "Trembling Lands," the marshy, dense wetlands that stretched from current-day Fort Atkinson, Wisconsin, and into the Northern Kettle Moraine area of Wisconsin provided a temporary veil to hide in. This area, a large question mark in historical accounts, was a meager refuge for the unprepared Native Americans.

For all the modern changes to the environment, there are still ancient dirt paths, lonely grave sites and ligneous river bends that provide glimpses of the spirit of the region formerly known as the Northwest Territory. The first European settlers left us with descriptions that hardly jive with the current landscape. An early map of the regions from 1829 notes that "a tenth is covered with timber, which grows in detached groves, the balance prairie. Springs of the purest water are to be found in abundance." It is difficult to stand under an overpass in present-day Davenport, Iowa, or the downtown Capitol Square in Madison, Wisconsin, and imagine a wilderness that could perplex a military force of between 3,000 and 4,500 troops.

The appeal of exploring the historical museums, wayside markers and parks relating to the Black Hawk War lies not only its historic significance and beautiful natural scenery but also in the amazing convergence of personalities that would later become cemented in American history. The Black Hawk War ushered in a young Abraham Lincoln's first successful election in 1832, to the post of captain in charge of his Illinois militia unit. It brought Black Hawk and future Confederate president Jefferson Davis face to face, as a young Davis escorted the imprisoned chief during his captivity at Rock Island. For one brief mustering, volunteer and enlisted army matched the population of any city in the Northwest Territories. (In 1830, Chicago's population was estimated at 100 souls; by 1840, it had grown to 4,470.)

If someone were anxious to cross off items on their bucket list, it would be technically possible to travel the entire Black Hawk Trail in one intensive daylong drive. By beginning at Rock Island, Illinois, and driving through Stillman, Illinois, across Wisconsin from Fort Atkinson, coursing through Wisconsin Heights and up to Victory and the final battle of Bad Axe, a road trip can be completed in about ten hours. However, that trip would provide you with just a cursory windshield view of ubiquitous interstate scenes followed by rolling hills anxious to share their story.

This travel guide will provide you with accessible day trips to explore, experience and discover the history of the Black Hawk War. There are communities that readily embrace their role in the conflict and host annual events that attempt to re-create the lifestyle and stories about the pioneer or "buck-skinning" era before statehood. Many businesses, communities and wayside sites resonate with the adoption of "Black Hawk" for their sports teams, businesses and attractions.

Also included are attractions, museums and sites in Chicago and the Lead Mining District around Mineral Point, Wisconsin; Dubuque, Iowa; and Galena, Illinois. While the full contingent of Black Hawk's followers didn't traverse to these locations, each played a pivotal role during the conflict and offer resources of interest for anyone taking up the journey. (The website www. blackhawktrail.com has links, updates and additional resources.)

FIRST NATIONS OF
THE OLD NORTHWEST TERRITORY

The Sauk and Fox Nations continue their traditions today. Sadly, the American government in the 1800s forcibly removed these communities either to lands outside of the heart of their traditional established communities or to the far western edge of their lands in today's central Iowa. The stories of the Sauk and Fox Nations are preserved, curated and honored at each of their three tribal lands in Iowa, Oklahoma and Kansas. The three federally recognized tribes welcome visitors and have invaluable visitors' centers that share their history, culture and traditions. The Meskwaki Settlement near Tama, Iowa, has annually held a large and inviting powwow for more than one hundred years. The tribal museum is the most accessible for people traveling through the Mississippi River Valley region.

While most of the museums, wayside markers and historic sites outside of tribal lands detailed in this book provide some information on the Sauk and Fox Nations, the descriptions are usually not from the viewpoint of the people from those tribes. The best resources are, of course, the tribal communities themselves.

The stories, tribulations and amazing culture of the Sauk and Fox Nations should be experienced by all Americans, and no examination of the Black Hawk War should be undertaken without exploring the resources the Sauk and Fox peoples wish to share.

A good starting point are the firsthand accounts from tribal members from the 1830s, including Black Hawk's autobiography. His account is still being reprinted, but digital versions of the original editions are available for free online. The interactions and speeches of key delegations between Native American and frontier leaders were often published in local papers. These exchanges provide important dialogues that demonstrate the struggle between indigenous people and the American government. Also of interest is the varied voices of the First Nation People that are collected in the archives of the newspaper the *Cherokee Phoenix and Indians' Advocate*.

Other newspapers during this era, including the *Sangamon Journal* (printed near Lincoln's home of New Salem, Illinois), are also digitized online and include some eye-opening articles translated from First Nation speeches among American leaders. The *Miner's Journal* and *Galenian*, which were printing in the lead mining region, also provide glimpses into the daily interests and happenings of the early settlers.

The writer Ray Young Bear, a member of the Meskwaki Tribe in Iowa, has shared powerful stories in his poetry and novels, which should also be consumed readily by all Americans but especially anyone living in the Mississippi River Valley.

SAC AND FOX TRIBE OF THE MISSISSIPPI IN IOWA (MESKWAKI)

The curated museum of the Meskwaki is a two-and-a-half-hour drive west of Dubuque, Iowa and an hour east of Des Moines, Iowa. The museum has welcoming staff who enjoy sharing stories and expanding on the amazing items on exhibit. The center is on tribal land, about one mile away from the large Meskwaki Casino and Convention Center. The lobby of the hotel in the convention center also displays unique cultural materials, as well as photographs of tribal members in traditional clothing and regalia. Lodging at the hotel is plentiful, although guests should book rooms early for the week of the very popular annual powwow in August. The settlement also maintains a large gift shop, conference center, hotel and casino.

CULTURAL CENTER AND MUSEUM
303 Meskwaki Road
Tama, IA, 52339
(641) 484-3185
meskwaki.org

Sac and Fox Nation of Oklahoma (Sa ki wa ki)

Sac and Fox National Public Library

The public is welcome to visit the exhibit cases and explore the resources and reference materials held at the central community building. Located five miles south of Stroud, Oklahoma, the thriving center promotes cultural exchanges and the continuation of the Sac and Fox traditions and language. Community events are shared through its website and online newsletter. An annual powwow at the Jim Thorpe Memorial Park has been welcoming the public since 1965. The Black Hawk Casino is directly across the highway from the community building.

920883 South Highway 99
Stroud, OK, 74079-5178
(918) 968-3526
sacandfoxnation-nsn.gov

Sac and Fox Nation of Missouri in Kansas and Nebraska (Ne ma ha ha ki)

Since 1996, the Sac and Fox Nation of Missouri in Kansas and Nebraska has hosted exhibits and a museum for the public. Interested individuals should contact the tribal offices to arrange a personal tour. There is no charge for access to the museum. The Nation's casino is located about thirty minutes away in Powhattan, Kansas.

Tribal Museum
305 North Main Street
Reserve, KS, 66434
sacandfoxks.com

Casino
1322 US Highway 75
Powhattan, KS, 66527-9624
(785) 467-8000

>>>><<<<

IN ADDITION TO THE Sauk and Fox Nations, other First Nation communities living in the Northwest Territory were also affected by the conflict. Each of the American Indian tribes in the region—from the Potawatomis to the Winnebagos, Kickapoos, Menomonees and Dakotas—has their own unique history and traditions. And each was also adversely affected by the removal policy of the United States. Within the Sauk and Fox communities, there were disagreements and factions that had varied strategies on how to deal with the demands of the U.S. government.

Additionally, there were communities that consisted of individuals not affiliated with a specific tribe. Prophetstown, located on the Rock River east of the Sauk and Fox communities, was a community of individuals who followed a charismatic leader, "The Prophet," who had a diverse lineage and background. This nonaffiliated group, numbering perhaps four hundred, was also displaced during the conflict. The village was incinerated early in the war before any shots were fired. There were also affiliations, family bonds and new traditions that remain immune to clear classification.

The early European pronunciation and spellings of First Nations in the Old Northwest Territory have numerous variants and can often be confusing. Many important distinctions between tribes and clans were often disregarded or ignored by early Americans.

FIRST NATION	FIRST NATION ETYMOLOGY	AMERICANIZED NAME OF TRIBE
Asakiwaki	Yellow Earth People	Sac or Sauk
Meskwaki	Red Earth People	Fox; Reynards (French)
Menominee	Wild Rice People; or The People	Menomonee
Ho Chunk	People of the Big Voice	Winnebago; Hoocaagra
Potowatomi	People of the Small Prairie	Mshkodésik
Kickapoo	Stands Here and There	Kickapoo
Dakota	Friend	Sioux
Báxoje	Grey Snow	Ioway; Iowa; Ayuhwa
Ojibwe	Puckered Moccasins	Chippewa

PRESIDENT ANDREW JACKSON'S INDIAN REMOVAL ACT OF 1830

The occasion will meet every man, when he must look inward, and make honest inquisition there. Let us beware how, by oppressive encroachments upon the sacred privileges of our Indian neighbors, we minister to the agonies of future remorse.
—Senator Theodore Frelinghuysen, 1830

What good man would prefer a country covered with forests and ranged by a few thousand savages to our extensive Republic, studded with cities, towns, and prosperous farms embellished with all the improvements which art can devise or industry execute, occupied by more than 12,000,000 happy people, and filled with all the blessings of liberty, civilization and religion?
—President Andrew Jackson, 1830

The First Nations throughout the Midwest and former Northwest Territory were summarily persecuted by the U.S. government. Each treaty and agreement that the United States confirmed, whether under duress or outright violence, would serve as just a temporary reprieve until the U.S. government had the resources to demand more land and more concessions and, ultimately, to force communities even farther west or south.

In March 1829, Andrew Jackson was inaugurated into office as the seventh president of the United States. After a turbulent election, the war hero of the Battle of New Orleans, businessman and slave owner secured a plurality of the electoral and popular vote. This included the three electoral votes of the state of Illinois. Jackson had served the United States beginning in the

Revolutionary War as a courier and also served during the War of 1812. Jackson was cognizant that a fair number of First Nations in the Northwest Territory had sided with the British during the War of 1812.

Tribal leaders including Black Hawk, Shabbona and Big Foot had been part of Tecumseh's alliance with the British during the War of 1812. Black Hawk had been active and successful in raiding American forces, especially on the Mississippi River. Shabbona, a member of the Ottawa tribe who became a Potawatomi chief, turned away from conflict with the United States after the War of 1812. He would espouse accommodation to the demands of the American government and actively warned American settlers of the oncoming conflict after the Battle of Stillman's Run.

Jackson's policy in 1830 was met with resistance. Sarah Wells, Frances Wilson, Catherine Norton and more than fifty other women from Steubenville, Ohio, petitioned the U.S. Congress against the Indian Removal Act. Their impassioned letter, which they admitted was written by a class of Americans who were not allowed to vote, implored their elected officials and constitutional guardians to protect the "undoubted natural right" of tribal members and to "save this remnant of a much injured people from annihilation, to shield our country from the curses denounced on the cruel and ungrateful, and to shelter the American character from lasting dishonour."

On April 9, 1830, Senator Theodore Frelinghuysen voiced his opposition to the proposed Indian Removal Act. His remarks set forth a reasoned yet emotional background on the subjugation of First Nations by American and European colonists:

> I insist that, by immemorial possession, as the original tenants of the soil, they [American Indians] hold a title beyond and superior to the British Crown and her colonies, and to all adverse pretensions of our confederation and subsequent Union. God, in his providence, planted these tribes on this Western continent, so far as we know, before Great Britain herself had a political existence. I believe, sir, it is not now seriously denied that the Indians are men, endowed with kindred faculties and powers with ourselves; that they have a place in human sympathy, and are justly entitled to a share in the common bounties of a benignant Providence. And, with this conceded, I ask in what code of the law of nations, or by what process of abstract deduction, their rights have been extinguished?
>
> Mere human policy, or the law of power, or the tyrant's plea of expediency, may have found it convenient at any or in all times to recede

from the unchangeable principles of eternal justice, no argument can shake the political maxim, that, where the Indian always has been, he enjoys an absolute right still to be, in the free exercise of his own modes of thought, government, and conduct.

Millions after millions he has yielded to our importunity, until we have acquired more than can be cultivated in centuries—and yet we crave more. We have crowded the tribes upon a few miserable acres on our Southern frontier; it is all that is left to them of their once boundless forests; and still; like the horse-leech, our insatiated cupidity cries, give! Give!

Every administration of this Government, from President Washington's have, with like solemnities and stipulations, held treaties with the Cherokees; treaties, too, by almost all of which we obtained further acquisitions of their territory. Yes, sir, whenever we approached them in the language of friendship and kindness, we touched the chord that won their confidence; and now, when they have nothing left with which to satisfy our cravings, we propose to annual every treaty—to gainsay our word—and, by violence and perfidy, drive the Indians from his home.

However reasoned and impassioned the women of Steubenville and the pleas of Senator Theodore Frelinghuysen and his allies were, their arguments fell on deaf ears. The American voting public, which in 1830 consisted only of white male citizens, had elected representatives and a president who were determined to displace the established First Nation communities in order for continued American expansion. The Indian Removal Act was approved by the Senate on a vote of 28 in favor and 19 against. The margin was narrower in the House of Representatives, with 101 in favor and 97 against.

President Andrew Jackson elucidated his thoughts on Indian removal during his inauguration speech. The soldier and politician set forth his administration's plans. Jackson had noted during his candidacy that it was his "sincere and constant desire to observe toward the Indian tribes within our limits a just and liberal policy, and to give that humane and considerate attention to their rights and their wants which is consistent with the habits of our Government and the feelings of our people."

However, after the passage of the Indian Removal Act, President Andrew Jackson detailed a starker path forward in his State of the Union address:

Can it be cruel in this Government when, by events which it can not control, the Indian is made discontented in his ancient home to purchase his lands, to give him a new and extensive territory, to pay the expense of his removal,

Above: Kee-o-kúk, the Watchful
Fox, Chief of the Tribe, on
Horseback, George Catlin,
1835. *Smithsonian American
Art Museum, Gift of Mrs.
Joseph Harrison Jr., object no.
1985.66.1A.*

Left: Wah-pe-kée-suck, White
Cloud (called the Prophet), Adviser
to Black Hawk, George Catlin,
1832. *Smithsonian American Art
Museum, Gift of Mrs. Joseph
Harrison Jr., object no. 1985.66.7.*

and support him a year in his new abode? How many thousands of our own people would gladly embrace the opportunity of removing to the West on such conditions! If the offers made to the Indians were extended to them, they would be hailed with gratitude and joy.

The story of the Cherokees' "Trail of Tears" is generally widely known with the American public. The broader scope of the effect the Indian removal policy had across the United States may not be fully told in communities and K–12 classrooms today. First Nations across the country would be systematically forced from their ancestral lands. It was not a singular action against the Cherokees, but rather a policy utilized by the federal government for decades against all First Nations.

The Illinois State Historical Society's *Atlas of Historic Tribes in Illinois (1673–1832)* describes the general geographic location of First Nations as reported from European explorers, including the Illiniwek, Maimi, Wea, Piankashaw, Fox, Sauk, Kickapoo, Mascouten, Delaware, Shawnee, Ottawa, Potawotomi and Winnebago tribes. Today in Illinois, there are no federally recognized First Nations in the entire state.

During the Black Hawk War, the governor of Illinois was John Reynolds. Reynolds spent his formative years growing up in the Illinois Territory. His family moved to Illinois Territory in 1800 to the then capital, Kaskaskia, on the shores of the confluence of the Kaskaskia and Mississippi Rivers. The twelve-year-old Reynolds witnessed the dramatic impact American settlement had on the landscape and on the established First Nation communities. In his autobiography, *My Own Times, Embracing also the History of My Life*, Reynolds described his family's experiences: "Among the high grass, and the wolves and wild animals howling and prowling about us every night. We enjoyed not the least semblance of a school, or a house of worship, or scarcely any other blessing arising out of a civilized community."

Reynolds estimated that during his childhood, the Illinois Territory was populated with about 800 Americans, about 1,200 French Creoles and perhaps 30,000 to 40,000 American Indians. He noted:

The Indian tribes inhabiting the wilderness of that day, which is now comprised in the present limits of the State of Illinois, were numerous, warlike, and courageous. The savages at that day possessed a wild and hostile spirit, that existed throughout the North American Indians. The Sac and Fox tribes were united and formed at that day a large, brave and powerful nation. Their chief residence was near Rock Island in the Mississippi,

*and throughout the country and that locality. The Winnebagoes resided
on the upper park of Rock River, and West of Green Bay, North West of
Lake Michigan, and on and over the Wisconsin River. The Pottawatomies
inhabited the region between Lake Michigan and the Illinois river, and
down that river. The war-like and courageous small nation of the Kickappo
Indians, dwelt in the prairies North and east of Springfield, and also in the
regions of country around Bloomington.*

Reynolds described additional tribes and their geography and notes in *My Own Times*: "[T]his day not one exists in the state. The destruction of the Indians of North America, is a subject that has enlisted the sympathy and deepest feeling of every philanthropist in the Union...generation succeeded generation of the natives, for ages in the peaceable possession of their inheritance descended from their ancestors, which gave them as much equity and justice to retain possession of it, as any civilized nation has, at this day for the country they inhabit....The wanton and wicked passion, existing in olden times in the hearts of the whites, to destroy and annihilate the natives, as if they were beasts of prey, has measurably subsided, and the spirit of kindness and Christianity has taken its place."

Reynolds's own actions during the Black Hawk War and throughout his administration implemented an unrelenting adherence to the Indian removal policy. The will of the influx of new settlers from the United States and Europe would hold precedence against the rights of the sovereign nations already located across North America.

Recognition of the older history of First Nations across the North American continent has slowly becoming more commonplace. A "Land Acknowledgement" statement has become a growing trend for many organizations, cities and colleges and universities to codify alongside their mission and vision statements. These statements openly note the names of the First Nations that had traditionally lived on the land prior to the arrival of Americans. The broad statements are often read at the start of public events and assemblies to show respect to the traditions that have been maligned or lost in American cultures. The University of Illinois has adopted this Land Acknowledgement statement:

*As a land-grant institution, the University of Illinois at Urbana–
Champaign has a responsibility to acknowledge the historical context in
which it exists. In order to remind ourselves and our community, we will
begin this event with the following statement. We are currently on the lands*

Three Fox Indians, George Catlin, 1837–39? *Smithsonian American Art Museum, Gift of Mrs. Joseph Harrison Jr., object no. 1985.66.19-21.*

of the Peoria, Kaskaskia, Peankashaw, Wea, Miami, Mascoutin, Odawa, Sauk, Mesquaki, Kickapoo, Potawatomi, Ojibwe, and Chickasaw Nations. It is necessary for us to acknowledge these Native Nations and for us to work with them as we move forward as an institution. Over the next 150 years, we will be a vibrant community inclusive of all our differences, with Native peoples at the core of our efforts.

I-o-wáy, One of Black Hawk's Principal Warriors, George Catlin, 1832. *Smithsonian American Art Museum, Gift of Mrs. Joseph Harrison Jr., object no. 1985.66.12.*

Early French and American settlers documented seventeen independent nations in Iowa. By 1851, all of these communities, except one, had either left or been removed through treaty negotiations.

In 2020, Iowa is home to one federally recognized First Nation: the Sac and Fox Tribe of the Mississippi in Iowa, also known as the Meskwaki, which translates to the "Red Earth People." The Meskwakis' endurance and fortitude to remain in Iowa are a unique instance of a tribe purchasing their own land. After numerous attempts to force the tribe out of Iowa, they persisted in returning to their homeland.

Today, Wisconsin recognizes eleven independent First Nations, but other First Nations have been removed from the state, including the Kickapoos and the Sauk and Fox. The Wisconsin state legislature enacted Act 31, or the "American Indian Studies in Wisconsin Act." The law required that "beginning September 1, 1991, as part of the social studies curriculum, include instruction in the history, culture and tribal sovereignty of the federally recognized American Indian tribes and bands located in this state at least twice in the elementary grades and at least once in the high school grades."

This act spurred a consortium of nonprofit and education partners to provide a robust collection of free curricular resources in a central website. Materials are organized at Wisconsin First Nations (www.wisconsinfirstnations. org) in order for "all school districts provide instruction in the history, culture, and tribal sovereignty of the American Indian nations in the state."

The Wisconsin State Historical Society has also made recent strides to engage with First Nation governments and integrate their wishes in their mission and priorities. The society unveiled a state-of-the-art preservation facility in Madison, Wisconsin, in 2019 that allows for First Nation members to have better access to their collections. The building incorporated an outdoor ceremonial space that was designed with feedback from the First Nation community.

The Wisconsin State Assembly formally apologized to the First Nation tribal governments of the Sauk and Fox Nations on May 10, 1989. The proclamation was read by State Representative David Clarenbach to about two hundred guests who assembled near the site of the Battle of the Bad Axe. While not in attendance, the chief of the Sac and Fox Nation of Oklahoma, Elmer Manatowa, marked the effort. The *Oklahoman* newspaper reported that Manatowa commented, "The Sac and Fox nation in Oklahoma is thriving. One hundred years ago, one might have thought the Sac and Fox might not be in existence today."

Wisconsin's proclamation reads in part:

> *Whereas; Chief Black Hawk responded to the suffering of his people by leading them back across the Mississippi in 1832 in the hopes of planting their crops and restoring their villages; and*
>
> *Whereas; there is no indication that Black Hawk had any intent to conduct military operations other than defense of his people on land he understood to be theirs; and*

31

Whereas; this affair was tragically concluded on August 1 and 2, 1832, when hundreds of unarmed women, children and elders were killed while crossing the Mississippi, what has come to be known as the Bad Axe Massacre, now therefore, be it

Resolved by the assembly, That the members of the Wisconsin state assembly express their regret and sorrow for the conduct of territorial militia drawn from within the boundaries of the present date state of Wisconsin; and, be it further

Resolved, That the assembly chief clerk communicate this sentiment to the appropriate tribal officials of the Sauk and Fox nations.

THE LEAD RUSH

Gray Gold in the Midwest

I have had occasion of late to pass frequently through town [Galena, Illinois]. *My olfactory nerves were scarcely more affected than they were from the exaltations which arose from the dead rats, old pork, beef, bacon, offal, etc., which lay in every part of the streets. Situated as we are without a police, every good citizen ought surely to feel it to be his duty, to observe the necessary degree of cleanliness.*
—*"Toby Scratch 'Em," letter to the editor,* Miner's Journal, *July 22, 1828*

Let them [the British Band] *now be taught a lesson which they will not forget quite so soon as they forget our treaties. And as lead is plentiful, and corn scarce, let them, this time, be brought to a reconciliation with us by paying them with our staple commodity.*
—*editorial,* Galenian, *May 2, 1832*

One of the first spirited financial panics in Europe was built around the fascination and promise of the European business interests along the Mississippi River. Occurring after the great Tulip Panic of 1637, the less remembered Mississippi Bubble took place in 1720. Speculators in France bought stock in a venture ballyhooed by John Law. In short order, Law had sold more than 650,000 shares to investors in his Compagnie des Indes, promising to bring the rich resources of the North American wilderness to European markets. The French control of the Mississippi River Valley was tenuous at that time. Within months, the company imploded, and shareholders were left with worthless shares. However, the dream of riches in the Midwest lingered.

Great riches were realized by the hardscrabble French fur traders, who relied on existing Native American commercial networks to establish trade routes across the Great Lakes. From Lakes Superior and Michigan to St. Louis, major corporate enterprises traded with First Nations to bring the bounty of the frontier to Europe. The Hudson Bay Company, American Fur Company and North West Company all plied their trading posts along the frontier.

By the early 1800s, a new resource had drawn the attention of American settlers. In 1805, Zebulon Pike noted in his journal a discussion with Julien Dubuque regarding his agreement with the local tribes and the Spanish monarchy to mine for lead. Pike estimated the annual amount of metal removed each year at between twenty thousand to forty thousand pounds.

Galena, Illinois—on the eastern side of the Mississippi River and south of the Wisconsin River—became the early center of mining activity in the newly established state. In 1822, the first two federal mining leases were awarded to Thomas D. Carmeal and Benjamin Johnson. That same year, Henry Schoolcraft (1793–1864) traveled throughout the region and made a detailed report of his findings in the Lead Region. He met with a Fox tribal leader at the Kettle village near the mouth of Catfish Creek near Dubuque. The tribe was smartly protective of sharing their knowledge of lead mines in the area. Schoolcraft noted that since Julien Dubuque's death, the tribes were worried that Americans would "encroach upon their right," so their practice was to "den[y] all former grants and did not make it a practice even to allow strangers to view their diggings." Schoolcraft persisted, and after bribing his contacts with more gifts, he was able to gain access to the mines. He then wrote about and shared the general locations of key mines in the region.

The boom at the lead mines in the Northwest Territory hit a bust in 1829. The trade of lead for supplies at markets in Galena and Mineral Point degraded to 25 percent of their prior buying power. The pressure put on the miners also affected the owners of the smelters, with reports of the first instances of the investors in smelters being unable to pay the tax they owed to the federal government. Changes in the administration of the regional superintendent from a veteran of the mining district to a new superintendent, Thomas Legate, brought new insecurity to the miners. While the miners and smelters had for years been content with paying their taxes in lead and working leased land, new arguments to open the land up to public sale were being proposed in the *Miner's Journal* in Galena:

> *Many, many individuals here left the mining country, who own lots and calculate never to return, and those lots, agreeable to the Superintendent's*

notice must lay idle. We would like to know why those individuals (who are transient persons too) should receive the protection of a government officer, when they, as SUCKERS, arrive in the spring and depart in the fall, draining the country of what little cash that's in it. Why not make them give blood and security to work their lots? And if they do not, let those who will, work them.

MANY MINERS.
Michigan Territory, October 20th, 1829

With depressed prices in lead continuing for the early part of the 1830s, the lead district may have been ripe for conflict. Caleb Atwater journeyed throughout the region in 1829 and met with many of the main mining operations, including Dodge's, Hamilton's and Gratiot's. According to Atwater, "These mines had been worked about three years, by, comparatively, but a few persons who were ignorant of the business they followed; and they labored under every disadvantage, yet they had manufactured more than 30 million pounds of lead."

The daily allotment for service in the militia was only $0.21 per day, or $6.30 per month, at the beginning of the Black Hawk War. While this paltry amount was somewhat better than nothing, it provided very little incentive for citizens to enlist. Since the mines were ostensibly shuttered during the panic of the conflict, it provided some remuneration but was much less than the going wage around Galena, estimated at $13 per month for mining. However, many miners also worked for the unlikely glimmer of hitting a lollapalooza. While not the norm, there were reports of lead runs that would bring in $3,000 over a year and a half, or $166 per month. The prospect of an easy jackpot kept many miners striving and dreaming through the daily dangers of their profession.

Masthead of the *Galenian* newspaper, published in Galena, Illinois, 1832.

The resolution of the Black Hawk War ushered in a new age for the Lead Region. President Jackson would open the land up to private sales in 1834. While there was a desire by the federal government to keep the lead mining properties within its control, many of those in charge of these early land sales of the lead mining region in what is today Wisconsin were corrupt. Henry Dodge and each of his sons were provided with opportunities to purchase large tracts of land around the area he had been mining illegally for years.

This privilege was also given to the three members of the First Territorial Convention from the lead district. Former superintendent Thomas Legate took the opportunity to invest in select lands he once administered and knew well. He purchased 1,540 acres and was able to sell them for a profit in 1845 for $8,400. The new superintendent, John Sheldon, also participated in the boondoggle. When a smelter approached Sheldon asking for the details on when the land he currently leased (and on which he had built a smelter) would be up for sale, Sheldon noted that it would be auctioned the following weekend. When the smelter lessee attended the auction, he learned that the lot had been purchased early in the week—by John Sheldon. Sheldon didn't have the means to purchase all of the lands that he was interested in, so he reached out to speculators who would finance his purchases. After President Jackson's term of office, Superintendent Sheldon was soon jettisoned from office. One federal officer noted that Sheldon had been acting as a king of a "vast mineral domain, and disposed of it as if it were indeed his own, uniform in only helping himself and his friends."

SLAVERY AND EARLY MINING EFFORTS

The role of slavery in the early mining industry is not often mentioned in the histories of the Northwest Territory. While slavery wasn't legal in the new territory and Illinois, Iowa, Wisconsin and Michigan never sanctioned slavery, Henry Dodge, James Estes, Moses Hickland and a handful of other owners were able to operate with slave labor at their mines due to the lack of any legal or judicial system on the frontier. The 1830 U.S. Census documents twenty-two male slaves and ten female slaves in Michigan Territory, all of whom lived in what is today Wisconsin. Slaves in the territory made up less than 1 percent of the 3,604 population, as noted in the 1830 census. The wealth of Henry Dodge was linked to the enslaved workers whom he brought with him from Kentucky to the Lead Mining District in 1828. According to the 1830 census, Henry Dodge's household included five slaves and four free Black individuals. Other mining operations saw the Northwest Territory as an opportunity to move out of slaveholding states. Henry Gratiot founded Gratiot's Grove and maintained a mining operation similar to Dodge's. Gratiot reportedly left Missouri due to his opposition to slavery. His mining operation employed five freed men and three freed women in 1830.

This early history of slavery in the Midwest is beginning to see further research by undergraduate students at the University of Wisconsin–Platteville. Under the guidance of Associate Professor Eugene Tesdahl, a cohort of students enrolled in the "African American Lead Miners, 1829–1890" course conducted new research into the lives of enslaved miners in the territory. They were able to determine the names of the male African Americans enslaved by Dodge: Lear, Joe, Tom, Jim and Toby. These individuals were given their freedom in 1838, and they adopted the surname of Dodge and remained for a time in the area. An exhibit of this research has been exhibited at the Mining Museum and Rollo Jamison Museum in Platteville, Wisconsin. One item included is this note from the June 16, 1830 *Miner's Journal*:

> *Runaway! On the night of the 6th instant, two negro men, one named Harrison, and the other Nimrod. Harrison is about 5 feet 4 inches high, between 25 and 27 years of age, of a very dark complexion, stout made, has a very flat nose, had on a pair of towline pantaloons and a blue broad cloth coat, worn out very much, and an old wool hat, and a pair of shoes, with nails in the heels and took with him an old yellow janes coat....$25 for the taking of either of them within the State, or $25 for taking of either confining or putting them in some jail, so we can get them. Joseph Boggs, D.P. Mahan, City of Jefferson, Missouri.*

A few weeks after the conclusion of the Black Hawk War, Colonel Charles Whittlesley described his travels through the mining district. He noted that "most of the improvements were of a temporary nature, consisting of a lead furnace and cabins." The miners were required to provide their ore to licensed smelters, who would then manage the process of removing the metal from the ore and would also pay the miners, as well as the 10 percent tax levied by the federal government.

Whittlesley noted that the smelting process involved was "simple and rapid. The furnace is a face wall, about two feet thick, located upon a gentle slope of the ground, with an arch or passage through the center; on each

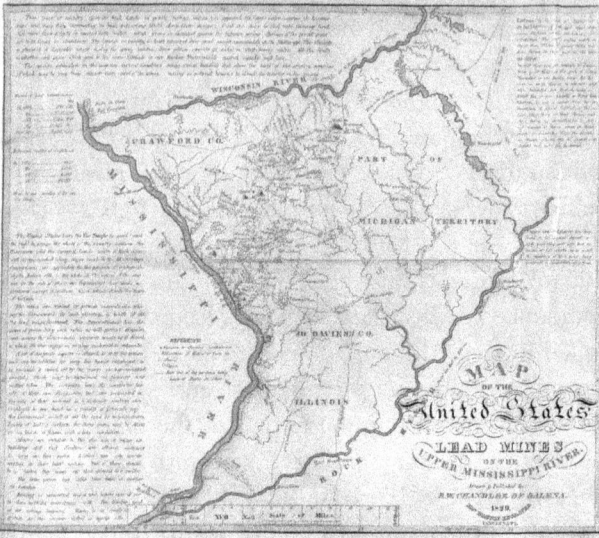

Map of U.S. lead mines on the upper Mississippi River, 1829. R.W. Chandler, Ebenezer Martin, engraver. *Courtesy of the Map Library at the University of Illinois at Urbana–Champaign.*

side of the arched opening, and in the rear or up-hill side, two wing walls run out traversely to the face wall, between which the wood is laid. The ore is placed upon it, and a continual fire kept up. The lead gradually separates from the dross, and runs into a cavity in front of the arch."

In 1832, the settlement of Helena was a growing community active in shipping lead down the Wisconsin River and ultimately to St. Louis. Helena was situated a few miles east of where Taliesin would later be built by Frank Lloyd Wright. Helena served an important role as the site of the first industrial building in Wisconsin: a shot tower. While a bustling shipping industry was sending the refined lead fresh from the smelters down to the Mississippi to St. Louis, there were no industries yet in place in the area that processed the lead into a finished product. The lead shot tower allowed for refined lead to be turned into a product ready for market. Instead of shipping the raw lead bars down the Mississippi River, the first manufacturer in Wisconsin was able to create a product that was readily in demand.

The production of lead shot from a tower is a simple and elegant solution to creating the small spherical shot used in guns. The molten lead would be poured through a screen at the top of the tower. Gravity and cooling worked their effects on the lead droplets as they fell from the top of the tower, creating the round lead shot. Any samples of shot that did not form to the right shape or size could simply be melted and sent back through the process.

LEAD MINING SITES AND MUSEUMS

THE MINING MUSEUM AND ROLLO JAMISON MUSEUM

The University of Wisconsin–Platteville has been the center for mining research and innovation for decades. With roots going back to 1836, the city has connections to one of the oldest institutions of higher education in Wisconsin. UW–Platteville merged in the 1900s with the Wisconsin Mining Trade School, which established the giant "M" on Platt Mound. Wisconsin's leadership in the manufacture of machinery for mining continues today with Milwaukee's Komatsu Mining Corporation.

The Platteville Mining Museum extrapolates on the science and long history of mining in the region. While the mine itself that resides underneath the museum is a more modern hole in the ground, the exhibits describe the mining techniques of Native Americans as well as the early miners in the Northwest Territory. Guests can tour the bowels of a drippy man-made cavern. The tour isn't for those with claustrophobic tendencies. The tour includes a ride in a working outdoor railroad gauge that was specifically run underground in area mines. The experience is nicely paired with the tour of Cave of the Mounds an hour east in Mount Horeb.

405 East Main Street
Platteville, WI, 53818
mining.jamison.museum

The Mining Museum and Rollo Jamison Museum entrance. Platteville, Wisconsin.

PENDARVIS: WISCONSIN HISTORICAL SOCIETY

Mineral Point was a major center of commerce during the Black Hawk War. With a population larger than Chicago's, the city was a trading center for settlers in the region. Today, Mineral Point boasts a historic downtown and numerous grand limestone and brick homes that preserve the frontier legacy. The town is always one decade away from being the next artistic commune in the tradition of Taos, New Mexico, or Pocatello, Idaho. Emigrants from Cornwall, England, played a leading role in the development of the city. Workers from Cornwall were adept in mining practices that allowed for deeper tunneling and are remembered today and celebrated through an annual Cornish Festival.

Over the past two centuries, many of the original lead mining buildings were dismantled or repurposed. During the 1930s, the Civilian Conservation Corps utilized the limestone from early structures for public works projects, including the municipal swimming pool. Two Wisconsin residents in the 1960s preserved and restored a selection of buildings that are part of the

Pendarvis is a restored mining settlement managed by the Wisconsin State Historic Site. Mineral Point, Wisconsin.

Pendarvis Historic Site, which is managed by the Wisconsin Historical Society. The tour of historic buildings and grounds provides a rich experience of the landscape that early American settlers inhabited.

114 Shakerag Street
Mineral Point, WI, 53565
pendarvis.wisconsinhistory.org

————

TOWER HILL STATE PARK: HELENA SHOT TOWER
Helena was a key river crossing and lead refining and shipping center. The community became a ghost town and is now a campground and state natural area. The shot tower has been reconstructed.

5808 County Road C
Spring Green, WI, 53588
dnr.wi.gov

————

MINERAL POINT LIBRARY AND ARCHIVES
137 High Street, second floor
Mineral Point, Wisconsin
(608) 987-2447
mineralpointlibraryarchives.wordpress.com

————

SHULLSBURG BADGER MINE AND MUSEUM
The hardscrabble life of a frontier miner is shared at the Shullsburg Badger Mine Museum. Shullsburg is home to some of Wisconsin's most authentic and distinctive cheesemakers, some of whom have benefited by using the abandoned caves in the area that were vestiges of the former mining industry. While the hills around Shullsburg look sturdy as far as hills go, one can't help but be amazed by how much of the earth and stone underneath the townsfolk have been removed. The museum features a tour of a mine shaft from the 1850s.

A few miles away from Shullsburg, William Hamilton, the son of Alexander Hamilton, was engaged in mining a claim. Hamilton's Diggings is now the community of Wiota and very near the site of the Battle of the Pecatonica.

279 Estey Street
Shullsburg, Wisconsin
badgermineandmuseum.com

————

IOWA COUNTY HISTORICAL SOCIETY
The local historical society's museum and visitors' center provides tourist information as well as advice on genealogical and historic sites in the area. The Wisconsin Historical Society includes in its collections a 196-pound lump of lead ore from nearby Ridgeway, Wisconsin.

1301 North Bequette Street
Dodgeville, WI, 53533
(608) 935-7694
iowacountyhistoricalsociety.org

————

THE NATIONAL MISSISSIPPI RIVER MUSEUM AND AQUARIUM
Along the shores of the Mississippi River, the National Mississippi River Museum and Aquarium successfully tells the story of the people who have called the area home, while incorporating the natural landscape and animals that also thrive in the Mississippi riverway. The center's many facets—as an aquarium, historical museum and environmental center—serve as a major regional attraction that encourages visitors to linger and enjoy the river, all while learning without effort. Guests are welcomed into the building with an introduction into the early Native American tribes that plied the rivers and made their homes along the waterways of the Mississippi River Valley. The museum connects the early Native American contact with French explorers and traces the development of the mines and growth of the area through European immigration. The museum incorporates living natural history lessons through zoological displays. Guests may enjoy aquatic exhibits of sturgeon, stingrays and alligator snapping turtles. Outdoor aviaries feature raptors, river otters and numerous other species that call the river home.

350 East Third Street
Port of Dubuque, IA, 52001
(800) 226-3369
rivermuseum.com

Governor Dodge State Park
4175 State Highway 23 North
Dodgeville, WI, 53533
(608) 935-2315

Black Hawk Lake Recreation Area
2025 County Highway BH
Highland, WI, 53543

FRONTIER FORTS, INDIAN AGENTS AND AGENCIES

The Agency House, "Cobweb Castle," as it had been denominated while lone the residence of a bachelor. It stood at what is now the south-west corner of Wolcott and North Water streets. Many will still remember it, a substantial, compact little building of logs hewed and squared. Around the Agency House were grouped a collection of log-buildings, the residences of different persons in the employ of the Government, appertaining to that establishment—blacksmith, striker, and laborers.
—*Juliette Kinzie,* Wau-Bun: The "Early Day" of the North-West, *description of the agency house in Chicago, 1832*

Indian Agencies...[are] the cause of excessive waste of Public Money. Along our frontier where there is the least necessity for an Indian Agency, there are U. States Troops, make each commander of such troops an Indian Agent. It is to be demanded of one who lives on the frontier, and knows the Indians, and the duties of their agents. Amongst these I class myself. That the commanding officer could perform this duty admits not of a doubt—he could perform it better. Let them be aware that enmity has not based one with towards the abolishment of Indian agencies—and I have taken this stand because I consider them an evil. [Signed]
Quod Erat Demonstrandum. *May 12, 1832.*
—*letter to the editor,* Galenian

enry Schoolcraft noted that an Indian agent's role was focused on "settling internal disputes between the tribes, fixing the boundaries to their respective territories, and thus laying the foundation of a lasting peace on the frontier." Agents, at best, were skilled in diplomacy, fluent in one or more Native American languages and proven professionals with experience in navigating the frontier. Unfortunately, many agents were appointed due to their corporate connections or familial ties. There are incidents of agents participating in rampant self-dealing and prioritizing personal enrichment over the rights of Native Americans.

The Indian agents sometimes served as friendly brokers but were more often interested in the corporate interests of major fur or trading conglomerates. Even agents who had some allegiance and sympathy for the tribes they were assigned to often used that influence to benefit themselves or the business interests they had associations with. As agents of the American government, they would work in tandem with political and military leaders to advocate for the westward expansion of the United States.

However, these federal employees often lacked the authority to implement federal laws. By 1828, Henry Dodge had established a major mining site in the Northwest Territory on land controlled by the Ho-Chunk Nation. Dodge had made his own personal side deal with the local tribe to be allowed to safely operate his mine. As Dodge's biographer noted, Dodge was confident that the writing was on the wall for the Native Americans in the Northwest Territory. Dodge knew that he would be better positioned to claim a stake in the new territory if he could be one of the first to establish a foothold.

John Marsh, the agent assigned to the area, noted that Dodge had "established twenty log houses in the immediate vicinity. He had a double furnace in constant operation, and a large quantity of lead in bars and the crude state. From the best information I have been able to obtain there are about one hundred and thirty men engaged in mining at this place, completely armed with rifles and pistols." When Marsh confronted Dodge and ordered him to leave the area, Dodge ignored him. The Indian agent had few options to enforce federal law against Dodge's illegal operation. Marsh reported his findings to his supervisor, Agent Joseph Street. Then Street, out of either a duty to law and his position or due to foolishness, suggested to Dodge that he should remove himself from his operation. Henry Dodge ignored Street and continued unabated.

During the start of the Black Hawk War, one of the most experienced American travelers and explorers was leading the Indian Agency. William Clark, the eponymous member of the famous William and Clark Expedition of 1804–6, would become America's great administrator in the West, stewarding numerous treaties and paving the way for the development of the North American frontier.

William Clark led the St. Louis Superintendency from 1822 to 1839. Reporting directly to the U.S. War Department, Clark oversaw the Native

American relations along the Missouri and Mississippi Rivers. Before the Black Hawk War, the local Indian agent for the Sauk and Fox at Rock Island was Thomas Forsyth, who had spent much of his life on the frontier and was well versed in the language and culture of neighboring American Indian communities.

Indian agents acted as arbiters between new American immigrants to the area and the resident Native American communities, as reported in this announcement by Indian agent Thomas Forsyth of Rock Island in the August 20, 1830 *Galenian*:

> *Notice is hereby given, that the Sack Indians found and delivered up to me the following described cattle, viz: A bay horse, no white about him, except some saddle marks, about thirteen hands high, seven or eight years old, said to be found some distance up Rock River. Four steers of the following description, said to be found west of Red Cedar River; one steer with a white back, belly and face, with redish sides.... The owner is requested to come forward, prove property and take them.*

Forsyth complained to his supervisor Clark against agents whom he saw as being corrupt. This whistle-blowing likely led to Forsyth's dismissal. Forsyth wrote a tragically prescient warning to Clark in 1830 that clearly outlined the volatile situation brewing between the Sauk and Fox Nations and the influx of American settlers.

Forsyth's half brother, John Kinzie, was the Indian agent for the Ho-Chunk Nation (Winnebago) and was situated north of the Four Lakes and Madison, Wisconsin region. In 1832, Kinzie was engaged in building his Agency House near Portage, Wisconsin. Kinzie was instrumental in working closely with the Ho-Chunk Nation in negotiating with their leadership to not join the British Band. A series of meetings during the summer was recorded, noting both Kinzie's and Henry Dodge's appeals to the Ho-Chunk. John Kinzie's wife, Juliette Augusta Magill Kinzie (1806–1870), wrote of their time in the Northwest Territory in her historic account, *Wau-Bun: The "Early Day" of the North-West*.

Forsyth was the Indian agent at the Sac and Fox Agency from 1818 until the summer of 1830. He was replaced by Felix St. Vrain, a member of a prominent business family in St. Louis. Marmaduke S. Davenport, one of the sons of George Davenport, was installed as the Indian agent on July 12, 1832, following St. Vrain's death during the conflict.

INDIAN AGENT HOUSES

HISTORIC INDIAN AGENCY HOUSE
Constructed during the summer of the Black Hawk War, the agency house's location and arrangement were directed by John Kinzie. The site is open to visitors during the summer months, and the local historical society manages periodic gatherings and programs.

1490 Agency House Road
Portage, WI, 53901
historicindianagencyhouse@gmail.com
agencyhouse.org

———

HISTORIC FORT SNELLING
Maintained by the Minnesota Historical Society, this seasonal site attraction includes community educational events and interpretive exhibits. Situated at the confluence of the Minnesota and Mississippi Rivers, the fort played a key role during the American war against the Dakotas and Ho-Chunks. The fort served as an internment camp for more than one thousand people and was the staging around for removal of Native Americans from the region.

200 Tower Avenue
St. Paul, MN, 55111
mnhs.org/fortsnelling

MILITARY FORTS

Established military forts and a hastily constructed redoubt were utilized by Americans as shelter during the Black Hawk War. While some of these structures were established military installations, many were haphazardly thrown together and were not maintained after the end of the war.

There was never a "Fort Atkinson" in the modern-day city of Fort Atkinson. In 1832, General Atkinson did lead the effort to construct a fort on the Rock River near the present-day city. This original fort was named Fort Cosconong (sometimes Coshkonong or Koshkonong), after the nearby lake. The location of Fort Cosconong has remained elusive to historians and academic archaeologists. While a plaque was affixed to a large boulder in front of one of Fort Atkinson's oldest and grandest homes proclaiming the general area of the lost fort, the actual site of the fort has not been found.

To make the issue even more confusing, there is an actual "Fort Atkinson" (named after General Atkinson) that was constructed in Iowa in 1840. This fort was constructed to continue to assist in the displacement of American Indians as they were pushed farther west and south. This fort became the namesake of the city of Fort Atkinson, Iowa. Both modern-day cities named Fort Atkinson have reconstructed frontier forts that are used for community events, including an annual rendezvous.

Fort Armstrong
Rock Island, IL
41.516447, -90.565636
Historic reconstruction near original site.

Fort Bingham—Blue Mounds
Blue Mounds, WI
43.017289, -89.831098
Archaeological research, no public access.

Fort Cosconong
Fort Atkinson, WI
42.925309, -88.858148
Historic reconstruction not on original site. Actual location of original fort unknown.

Fort Crawford
Prairie du Chien, WI
43.057171, -91.159276
Built on the site of Fort McKay and Fort Shelby, 1814. Reconstructed partial fort at Villa Louis Historic Site.

Fort Crawford Rebuilt
Prairie du Chien, WI
43.042644, -91.148473
Site of Black Hawk's imprisonment. Museum and original footings open to the public.

Fort Sinsinawa—Jones
Hazel Green, WI
42.523203, -90.546996
No marker. May have been at the entrance of today's Sinsinawa convent.

Fort Dearborn
Chicago, IL
41.89011223, -87.62453606
Plaque on Michigan and Wacker Streets mark the former site.

Fort Defiance
Mineral Point, WI
42.796354, -90.129416
Roadside plaque.

Fort Dixon
Dixon, IL
41.846513, -89.48472
North side of Rock River, near Dixon's Ferry. Statue of Lincoln in militia garb and Dixon's cabin reconstruction.

Fort Winnebago
Portage, WI
43.555056, -89.43353
Two original buildings; summer programs.

Fort—Apple River
Elizabeth, IL
42.318089, -90.214492
Reconstructed walled structure and buildings. Museum and visitors' center.

Fort Union
Dodgeville, WI
42.916083, -90.117951
Historic plaque.

Fort Jackson
Mineral Point, WI
42.85897, -90.177105
Historic plaque near downtown historic district.

Fort Howard
Green Bay, WI
44.473211, -88.029987
Actual location unknown. Buildings from original site moved to Heritage
Hill Historic Park.

Fort Gratiot
Gratiot Grove, WI
42.551781, -90.232753
No buildings remain, but an 1835 home built by Gratiot is near the original fort.

Fort Johnson
Warsaw, IL
40.37049, -91.405022
Archaeological site on private land. No visitor access.

Fort Mackinac
Mackinac, WI
45.851593, -84.616275
Wisconsin State Historic Site and Museum.

Fort Malden
Amherstburg, ON, Canada
42.108364, -83.113399
National Historic Site.

Fort Snelling
Saint Paul, MN
44.890937, -93.182942
Historic site, tours and visitors' center.

Fort Wilbourn
La Salle, IL
41.311526, -89.088015
Roadside plaque.

Jefferson Barracks
St. Louis, MO
38.511923, -90.279699
Historic site, museum and programs.

THE NORTHWEST TERRITORY WILDERNESS

Stopped at some islands [on the Mississippi River south of Rock Island]
*where there were pigeon-roosts, and in about 15 minutes my men had knocked
on the head and brought on board 298* [pigeons]. *The most fervid imagination
cannot conceive their numbers. Their noise in the woods was like the continued
roaring of the wind, and the ground may be said to have been absolutely covered
with their excrement. The young ones we killed were nearly as large as the old;
they could fly about ten steps, and were one mass of fat; their craws were filled
with acorns and the wild pea. They were still reposing on their nests, which were
merely small punches of sticks joined, with which all the small trees were covered.
Met four canoes of the Sacs, with wicker baskets filled with young pigeons. The
expeditions of Zebulon Montgomery Pike to headwaters of the Mississippi River,
through Louisiana Territory, and in New Spain.*
—*William Baily (1828–1861), in 1875 describing in* Our Own Birds *his
witnessing of a migration of passenger pigeons*

In 1832, the landscape, vegetation and wildlife were starkly different in the
states we now call Iowa, Wisconsin and Illinois. The landmarks today—of
buildings, interstates, cities and silos—were nonexistent. The great prairies
were yet to be broken by pioneers into pliable croplands. The islands of
communities, established over centuries by Native Americans, had not made
the same impact that the oncoming migration of Europeans and Americans
would bring in the 1830s.

Wisconsin writer Ben Logan (1920–2014) wrote how as a child he always kept an eye out, hoping against hope that he would come across a surviving passenger pigeon. Unfortunately for Logan, the last captive pigeon passed away in 1914.

In September 1832, Colonel Charles Whittlesley of Eagle Harbor captured his travels through the Four Lakes area, near today's Madison, Wisconsin. He described the landscape north of the Wisconsin River, near the hills of Baraboo:

> *In the spacious valleys that intervene, millions of small flowers mingle their bright colors with the green of meadows, chastening and ruralizing the scene. An excitable person would exclaim at the sublimity of such a prospect, having the grandeur of a mountain without its loftiness, and the command of the sea without its monotony. A painter would pass from the grand outlines and dwell with delight upon the beauty of its details.*
>
> *We started a plenty of grouse, and frequently saw deer quietly feeding on the hill sides, secure from our rifles in the distance. The sight of a prairie wolf was not an uncommon thing. This animal differs materially from the common wolf, being less in size, of a gray color and wanting in speed.... Their uniform practice is to regard to us, after running away at a moderate step a couple hundred yards, was, to face about and examine the company.*

Caleb Atwater traveled from St. Louis and up the Mississippi River to Prairie du Chien in 1829 and attended the great gathering of First Nations. He traversed the Lead Mining Region and crossed overland from Helena, Wisconsin, through Dodgeville and south to Galena, Illinois.

Atwater likened the summer environment and air quality to that of Italy. He noted that the visibility was so clear he was able to see clearly over a span of at least fifty miles, from Dodgeville to Gratiot's Grove. The climate seemed to encourage good health among the citizens, with only one person he met being in poor health. That one sickly person was one of Henry Dodge's daughters, who brought her preexisting condition with her from Missouri. However, Atwater did run into a few people whose lungs had been negatively affected by their employment in the lead furnaces.

Atwater detailed his interactions with the native wolves (or possibly coyotes):

> *The prairie wolf, in size, color and disposition, is half way between the black wolf and the gray fox. His food consists of almost every thing within his reach—grasses, birds, and their eggs—pigs and poultry. He can live on*

grasshoppers, crickets and bugs—he can steal from a hen coop, or a barn yard, and when pinched with hunger, he will even venture into a kitchen and steal a crust of bread. He often approached a few feet of me, at night, when I lay out on the prairie, and barked at me with great earnestness.

The most well-known American description of the Northwest Territory may be from Laura Ingalls Wilder (1867–1967) of her family's homestead in Pepin, Wisconsin, about one hundred miles north of the Battle of the Bad Axe. Her novels were written as reminiscences when she was in her eighties, and Laura was assisted by her daughter, Rose Wilder (1886–1968). Her novels vividly evoke the danger the wilderness of the untamed Northwoods held for the family. The popular books have been adapted into television series, but the familiar stories received criticism in the twenty-first century for negative depictions of Native Americans. The American Library Association decided in 2018 to no longer honor the author by removing her name from the annual Children's Literature Legacy Award, which had been named in honor of Wilder since 1954.

The *Miner's Journal* of September 13, 1828, described the area of the Lead Region:

Good farming land; and might support dense population was it not for the scarcity of timber-about four-fifths of the whole being prairie.

The timber consisting principally of oak, and a small portion of aspen and hickory in generally found upon the high land....The frequent firing of the prairies, has rendered the timber, in a great measure, scrubby, very little being found fit for rails or building, except in the groves along the Mississippi. This tract of country is as well watered perhaps, as any other in the United States. Hardly a square mile can be found anywhere without abundant springs of the purest water, except indeed upon the main dividing ridges and a tract from the portage running towards the heads of Rock River and the Cos-co-hone or River of the Four Lakes.

Newspapers of the day often included front-page alerts of amazing animal reports. The *Miner's Journal* of August 23, 1832, noted that a man had caught a six-foot-long rattlesnake with twenty-three rattles on its tail and a badger within the snake's belly.

Today, the wildlife around Rock Island and Black Hawk's former home of Saukenuk once again include bald eagles as well as flocks of majestic white pelicans.

In the "Trembling Lands," the inhospitable marshlands north of the Rock River that confounded General Atkinson, you will find that a good deal of the landscape has been tamed and drained. Farmland and cities now prosper in a region that once easily obscured more than 1,200 people for weeks.

Vestiges of the Trembling Lands can still be witnessed, even if the scale and solitude of the wilderness of 1832 is long gone. More than three thousand acres of marshland and tamarack swamp that were too entrenched to drain remain in Jefferson County, Wisconsin. Summer hikes across this landscape, especially on a hot and humid days in July or August, provide a rich, fragrant and solitary experience.

EFFIGY AND CONICAL MOUNDS

Visitors to downtown Lake Geneva, one of Wisconsin's most visited tourist communities, will pass by an area where two large effigy mounds that were described as "lizard" shaped once resided. The massive forms of the effigy mounds were fifty to eighty feet long, ten to twelve feet wide and two to three feet high. The heads of each lizard sloped toward the lake with outstretched arms and legs. Many of the effigy mounds that American settlers encountered became victims to development and civilization, including these two lizard mounds and others documented along Geneva Lake.

Effigy and conical mounds were constructed across the Midwest, especially along the river valleys from Ohio, west through Iowa and north from Minnesota down the Mississippi River Valley to St. Louis. These earthen works are priceless cultural artifacts. Created from about 1200 to 600 BCE, they serve as resilient guideposts to the people who once lived and thrived in today's Midwest. Conical mounds are generally simple geometric shapes, typically round or oval. Effigy mounds are constructed in the shape of animals or figures.

Many of the mounds were destroyed during the influx of settlers in the 1800s. Federal and state laws protect the mounds today, but encroachment by development and commercial interests still threaten them. Notable archaeological grounds, effigy and conical mounds are located alongside key sites of the Black Hawk War.

Conical and Effigy Mound Sites and Museums

Effigy Mound, National Monument

Across the Mississippi from Prairie du Chien in Iowa is the treasure of the national park. The visitors' center boasts important displays of the First Nation history in the area. This includes artifacts of the First Nation communities, archaeology and the trade routes along the Mississippi. In addition to the exhibits, there is a regularly updated informational video. The park rangers are very knowledgeable about the site and area.

A convenient forest and marsh path directly outside the visitors' parking lot is available for visitors who have only a few hours to spend at the park. Visitors who want to experience the rare and amazing effigy mound groups should plan ahead and prepare to bring appropriate hiking gear. While the trails are not technically difficult, guests should arrive ready for seasonal conditions.

151 IA-76
Harpers Ferry, IA, 52146
nps.gov

———

Aztalan State Park

Not far from the Trembling Lands, where the Black Hawk Band lingered during the summer of 1832, lies the important Cahokian city of Aztalan. Situated on the Crawfish River, a tributary of the Rock River, Aztalan was a major settlement. A major central pyramidal mound and fortifications have been restored.

N6200 County Road Q
Jefferson, WI, 53549

———

Lake Mills Aztalan Historical Society
N6284 Highway Q
Jefferson, WI, 53549
lakemillsaztalanhistory.com

———

INDIAN MOUND PARK
This is a free walking trail along a series of thirteen effigy and conical mounds, shaped like mink, panther, turtle and thunderbird. The city of Whitewater, home of the University of Wisconsin's Whitewater Warhawks, manages a park with a grouping of conical mounds. While the majority of extant mounds are near water features, these are not near a river, lake or creek.

288 South Indian Mound Parkway
Whitewater, WI, 53190
whitewater-wi.gov

———

INTAGLIO MOUND
One of the rarest extant effigy mounds is an incised mound that is carved into the landscape. This intaglio panther mound is along the Rock River in Fort Atkinson on Highway 106. The mound is just a few blocks away from the reconstructed Fort Koshkonong.

1230 WI-106
Fort Atkinson, WI, 53538

———

BELOIT COLLEGE
The campus is built around a series of conical mounds and one effigy mound. History on the background and research of the mounds is available at the Logan Museum.

700 College Street
Beloit, WI, 53511
beloit.edu

———

INDIAN MOUNDS AND TRAIL PARK, LAKE KOSHKONONG
A remnant of the ancient foot trail established by American Indians and a few remaining mounds are accessible near the Koshkonong Country Club.

The golf course and clubhouse are situated on a rise along the eastern edge of a widening of the Rock River that was a popular harvest and hunting area.

W7561 Koshkonong Mounds Road
Fort Atkinson, WI, 53538

RIVERS AND WATERWAYS

The river is rich in Indian history and traditions. Black Hawk's was once a puissant name hereabouts; as was Keokuk's, further down. Black Hawk adopted the ways of the white people, toward the end of his life; and when he died he was buried near Des Moines.
—Life on the Mississippi, *Mark Twain*

This river [Wisconsin] *is the grand source of communication between the lakes and the Mississippi, and the route by which all the traders of Michilimackinac convey their goods.*
—*Zebulon Pike, 1806*

Wa-Po-Na, the principal chief of the Fox nation remained several days in this town [Galena] *during the last week, on his return to the Indian village at Du Buque's mines. During his stay here he sat for his portrait at Mr. Berry's rooms. He was dressed in fine style. Wa-Po-Na resides on the Rock River, is much respected by the Americans, and universally revered by his nation.*
—Miner's Journal, *July 25, 1828*

T he waterways of the Mississippi River Valley served as the highways for Native American people for centuries before the arrival of European settlers. Important permanent communities and seasonal gathering grounds followed the riverways. From the confluence of the Mississippi and Rock Rivers, the Sauk and Fox had established towns that served their people for generations. These established communities would serve as the groundwork for the European establishment of trading posts and forts from Green Bay to Prairie du Chien and along the length of the Mississippi.

Henry Rowe Schoolcraft described the beauty of his travels from Prairie du Chien up the Wisconsin River toward Portage:

> *The river itself is almost a moving mass of white and yellow sand, broad, clear, shallow, and abounding in small woody islands, and willowy sandbars....We put ashore for dinner, in a very shaded and romantic spot. Poetic images were thick about us. We sat upon mats spread upon a narrow carpet of grass between the river and a high perpendicular cliff... Overhanging trees formed a grateful bower around us. Alas, how are those to be pitied who prefer palaces built with human hands to such sequestered scenes. What perversity is there in the human understanding, to quit the delightful and peaceful abodes of nature, for noisy towns and dusty street.*

Today, most travelers will glide over bridges crisscrossing the Mississippi, Wisconsin and Rock Rivers without a second thought of the water coursing along below them. The rivers and waterways were the first and most important lines of commerce, communication and civilization.

The ancient city of Aztalan was established on the Crawfish River, a branch of the Rock River. The weirs they built to catch fish along the edges of Aztalan are still visible during low water conditions.

Traveling along the river today may provide the most visceral and immediate natural exposure. Local canoe and inner tube rentals are readily available across the Wisconsin and Rock Rivers and lakes region of southern Wisconsin and northern Illinois. More refined to outright first-class touring options are also available along the Mississippi.

THE ROCK RIVER NATIONAL WATER TRAIL

In the summer and fall, river enthusiasts flock to the Rock River and its tributaries. Pontoons ply the waters of Lake Koshkonong, and numerous restaurants maintain piers to welcome hungry river-goers. More than three hundred miles of river trails welcome kayakers, canoeists and tubers. An active volunteer group of nature and river enthusiasts has helped to maintain, promote and preserve the river. This group's efforts led to the area being designated as a National Water Trail in 2010. Detailed information on access and water conditions is available on its website (rockrivertrail.com/water-trail).

The *Celebration Belle*

Headquartered out of Moline, Illinois, one of the Quad Cities, the *Celebration Belle* has a variety of one- to two-hour excursions and day-long journeys between key cities. You can spend one full day between Dubuque, Iowa, and the Quad Cities or combine multiple day trips to journey as far north as Prairie du Chien, to see longer stretches of the Mississippi. The three-level-plus rooftop ship includes regular commentary by the ship's captain, as well as unparalleled views of wildlife and river bluff scenery. The Mississippi River remains an active shipping route, with barges steering tons of materials up and down the river. Longer excursions provide opportunities to go through one or more of the locks maintained by the Army Corps of Engineers. While the river has been tamed, traveling by boat on the Mississippi River still provides an excellent opportunity to see the country from a unique perspective.

2501 River Drive
Moline, IL, 61265
(800) 297-0034
celebrationbelle.com
info@celebrationbelle.com

———

American Queen Steamboat Operating Company

The "Cadillac" of riverboat experiences on the Mississippi River is provided by the American Queen Steamboat Operating Company. The massive, first-class vessels provide unmatched luxury experiences for travel from the mouth of the Mississippi to the Twin Cities. The company's vessels ply the waterways of North America, and while you may need the expense account of Mark Twain to book passage, the experience of staying on a four-star floating hotel is one you won't soon forget.

222 Pearl Street
New Albany, IN, 47150
americanqueensteamboatcompany.com

———

LA CROSSE QUEEN
North of the final battle at the mouth of the Bad Axe River, the *La Crosse Queen* provides one-and-a-half-hour to three-hour cruises on the fifty-passenger, two-level ship.

405 East Veterans Memorial Drive
La Crosse, WI, 54601
lacrossequeen.com

————

CHESTNUT MOUNTAIN RESORT
Galena's ski resort operates a seasonal weekend tour on the weekends. The twenty-five-person pontoon boat operates one-and-a-half-hour tours. The resort is about a half hour from Galena and is situated near a strikingly beautiful section of the Mississippi and Fever Rivers.

8700 West Chestnut Mountain Road
Galena, IL, 61036
(800) 397-1320

GEOGRAPHIC MOUNDS AND HIGH POINTS

Some of these mounds are three miles in circumference, at their bases, and three hundred feet in height. These lofty elevations serve as land marks, which, being perfectly well known to the people of this region, not only by name, but in appearance. With one or more of them being in sight, no one ever loses his way, when traveling in the country of the lead mines.
—Caleb Atwater, 1829

With the assistance of these natural beacons, & knowing the locality, a perfect stranger may travel all through the country, with the same confidence of finding the object of his journey, that an experience mariner traverses the ocean with the assistance of a chart in search of some foreign port.
—Miner's Journal, September 13, 1828

Lost Rocks. Scattered over the surface of our prairies, are large rocks, of granite formations, roundish in form, usually called by the people lost rocks. *They will weigh from one thousand to ten or twelve thousand, and are entirely detached, and frequently found several miles distant from any quarry. It is a curious question, and one which has elicited some attention from thinking men.*
—Galenian, May 16, 1832, an early description of "glacial erratics," or large boulders transported and then deposited by retreating glaciers

For anyone who has traveled outside of the Great Plains or the Midwest, it may seem a stretch of the imagination to call the rolling hills and ridges of Northern Illinois, Eastern Iowa and Southwest Wisconsin mountainous. To American settlers, the terrain across the Driftless area and Lead Region were often lauded for their mountain-like qualities. Key mounds—including the Platt Mounds outside present-day Platteville and the two Blue Mounds west of Mount Horeb—served as important wayfinding landmarks.

Early French and American explorers interpreted the Ho-Chunk (Winnebago) name for the hills in the Driftless area north of the Wisconsin River as the Ocooch Mountains. This "mountain" range runs roughly north of the Wisconsin River from Sauk Prairie to Prairie du Chien and north to La Crosse and consists of the most elevated peaks and deep valleys in the state. Wisconsin writer Ben Logan mused that dairy farmers who knocked a pail down one hill would have to chase the bucket for miles, as it would continually roll up one hill and down the next, creating a perpetual natural rollercoaster. The last pursuit of the Black Hawk War took place in this most untamed and vertically challenging area. The *Galenian* described the territory as "one continued series of mountains. No sooner had they reached the summit of one high and almost perpendicular hill than they had to descend on the other side equally steep to the base of another. Nothing but a deep ravine, with muddy banks, separated these mountains. The under bushes were chiefly thorn and prickly ash."

An article from the *Miner's Journal*, printed in Galena on September 9, 1828, provides a striking description of the landscape that could be viewed from the top of the Blue Mound in the years leading up to the conflict:

A Visit to the East Mound
It was on one morning in the latter end of the month of August, when we set out, four in number, from Dodgeville, in the south-west corner of the territory of Michigan, to pay a visit to a very magnificent mound, which is so large and high, that it can be seen from all directions, as far as the eye can discern, and viewing it from a great distance it assumes the appearance of a sky blue cloud; which has given in the name "Blue Mound." The day was unusually warm, the mercury in the thermometer standing at 92 deg. Fahrenheit, and the sky was clear, when we proceeded onward. When within about 2 miles distance from the base of the highly interesting object of our visit, night came upon us; and finding a cabbin [sic] near a small hill, we entered and found it inhabited by very hospitable people, who welcomed us till morning; when we again set out, and soon found ourselves at the foot

of the Mound. After resting our horses a short time, we proceeded to ascend the lofty pile in order to reach the summit; which we soon accomplished, by taking a special direction around the hill, till we found ourselves upon the most elevated point of the mound.

We then halted and took a general and perspective view of all the various scenes around us, till our sight grew dim by the long continuance of variegated scenes presenting one after another, till it appeared as if we could see the whole creation before us. Up on one hand could be seen the high and stupendous bluffs of the rapid Ouisconsin, nearly from its source to its mouth, while on the other, could be seen the distant high lands bordering on Rock River; there we could view the beautiful rivers Pickatolica and Platte, and at the distance of about 60 miles, could be seen the mountainous bluffs of the great Mississippi River; all which presented so sublime and majestic scenes as to require more than human art to describe, or human intellect to conceive.

In almost all directions, except the north and east, was seen the smoke of the Lead Furnaces, and now and then a wandering human being in search of his fortune, by digging in the earth for Galena [lead ore]. At length, our eyes being weary with viewing scenes so remote, where nothing but distance obstructed our vernal extension, we descended from the lofty summit of this supposed work of art to its base; thence returned to a beautiful little hamlet, delightfully situated on a rolling prairie near a beautiful spring branch, where we found a new Inn, built and kept by J. Carman.

I leave now, for the reader to make his own reflections, after informing him, that one year ago, there were no human beings within 50 or 60 miles of this place, except some wandering natives of the forest in pursuit of game. The rapid association of ideas which must go on in the mind of every one who travels that way, are calculated to execute wonder and admiration, and cause him to inquire, what aspect will this country assume 20 years hence?

AMBULATER

What aspect will visitors today, almost two hundred years since American settlement, be inspired by when they visit the Blue Mounds? And what will that view inspire in guests two hundred years from now?

PLATT MOUND: THE WORLD'S LARGEST "M," OUTSIDE PLATTEVILLE, WISCONSIN
The Walt Disney Corporation was so impressed with Platteville's dedication to its giant "M" that in 1998 the community won a national competition to host a celebration of Mickey Mouse's sixtieth birthday. The giant white "M" that

is arranged across the west side of Platt Mound was conceived by the student body in 1939 at the University of Wisconsin–Platteville. The arrangement of stones painted white across the mound honors the mining tradition of the area and the school's mascot, a miner named Pioneer Pete. The trail to the peak of the mound is accessible via a few parking spots on Mound Road.

———

PLATT MOUND TRAIL
19521 West Mound Road (just past intersection of City B)
Platteville, Wisconsin

———

BLUE MOUNDS, WISCONSIN
In Southwest Wisconsin, the rolling hills of the Driftless area have been poetically described by Wisconsin luminaries and authors. The landscape inspired Frank Lloyd Wright, Georgia O'Keeffe and August Derleth and attracted innumerable visitors to see the faraway rolling hills for themselves. The Blue Mound was a key landmark during the Black Hawk War.

Many residents and visitors to the Midwest may be familiar with the ubiquitous and well-designed logo for the Cave of the Mounds State Park, a popular tourist attraction literally within the Blue Mounds. The icon of the state park, a blue "M" shape with a red circle in the center of the letter, has been the logo used by the park in its advertising and billboards throughout Wisconsin and Illinois. While not discovered until 1939, this National Natural Landmark remains remarkably pastoral, except for a few forlorn cellphone towers.

———

BLUE MOUND STATE PARK
Access to the park requires a small daily fee or the purchase of an annual Wisconsin State Park sticker. The observation tower provides guests a commanding view of the Driftless area. Open year-round.

4350 Mounds Park Road
Blue Mounds, WI, 53517
(608) 437-5711

Cave of the Mounds
2975 Cave of the Mounds Road
Blue Mounds, WI, 53517
(608) 437-3038

Mines of Spain, Dubuque, Iowa
The earliest mining collaboration between Julien Dubuque and the Sauk and Fox Nation took place at the Mines of Spain. While the Spanish king was never able to effectively control the area, early European *voyageurs* struck agreements with American Indian communities to harvest the malleable metal. The park is free and boasts numerous trails, as well as a worthwhile vista of the Mississippi River Valley.

E.B. Lyons Interpretive Center
8991 Bellevue Heights Road
Dubuque, IA, 52003
minesofspain.org

Bald Bluff, La Grange, Wisconsin
The Southern Unit of the Kettle Moraine is a popular biking, hiking and cross-country skiing area. The peak of Bald Bluff was the site of General Atkinson's camp in July 1832 for a few nights. The peak is a short, steep walk from the parking lot off County H, a few miles north of the intersection of County H and Highway 12. The bluff is about 1,050 feet high and provides excellent views. A glacial erratic, the "stone elephant," is about a mile farther down the path from the peak of Bald Bluff. This hike is part of the Ice Age Trail. Visit the website for more nearby hiking options.

BIKE PATHS, THE OLD MILITARY ROAD AND ROADSIDE MARKERS

*There is no difficulty if you keep a little to the north and strike the great Sauk
trail. If you get too far to the south, you will come upon the Winnebago Swamp,
and, once in that, there is no telling when you will ever get out again. Be sure
you get on the great track that the Sauks have made, in going every year from the
Mississippi to Canada to receive their presents from the British Indian Agent.*
—*Mrs. Dixon providing directions to Chicago from Dixon's Ferry, in* Wau-Bun

From Edward's Trace to the Old Stage Coach Trail and from Chicago to
Galena, the terrestrial paths across the Northwest Trail were usually built
on the worn trails created over generations by First Nation communities.
The "Sauk Trail" was a path that wound its way from Rock Island, Illinois,
to the British Fort Malden, across the Detroit River into Canada. This nearly
450-mile journey was traveled each year by Sauk and Fox leaders to meet
with their British allies. The route was used since before 1812 up through at
least the start of the Black Hawk War. Remnants of these original roads are
noted on worn roadside plaques and interstate waysides.

For decades, historic societies have utilized roadside markers to educate,
engage and provide visitors with an opportunity to take a break from driving.
Local historians have attempted to master the fickle art of describing
historical events with a limited amount of sign space, while also hedging
against the ever-changing sensibilities of the general public. While dozens
of roadway signs follow the roadways of Wisconsin and Illinois, a map of
locations with their description is included at the end of this book.

On May 2, 1832, the *Galenian* newspaper, whose motto was "Let Us Support the Interest of Our Own Country and She Will Support Ours," printed a news release from the U.S. War Department: "As the country is inhabited by tribes of savages, who have ever been, and still are hostile in their feelings and disposition towards the people of the United States, a road…appears not only necessary as it regards the transportation of troops and military stores, but to the protection of the white population." This new road would connect Fort Howard in Green Bay to Fort Crawford in Prairie du Chien via Fort Winnebago near the portage. While the road would not be completed until after the war, the Military Road would lay the groundwork for Wisconsin's highways.

Old Military Ridge Trail Bicycle Path

The conflicts between American immigrants to the Midwest and the resident First Nations pushed the American settlers to clamor for a civilized road so that they could properly and safely travel across the territory.

While most of the original route has been re-oriented and altered since the 1830s, the name still remains. A major bicycle route from Verona to Dodgeville, Wisconsin, the Military Ridge Trail approximates the ridge of the old Military Trail Road. The trail in Wisconsin shouldn't be confused with the similarly named Military Road in Iowa, which connects Iowa City to Dubuque. A plaque in downtown Dubuque commemorates this road.

From Verona to Dodgeville, with connecting segments that reach into Madison and Blue Mound State Park, this popular bicycle path is a good option for a long day trip or to explore in shorter segments. An annual fee sticker is required to use the trail, available at the trailheads in Verona or Dodgeville or at a self-serve kiosk in Blue Mounds, Barneveld or Ridgeway.

2565 Old County Road
Verona, WI, 53593

DNR Dodgeville Service Center
322 North Douglas Street
Dodgeville, WI, 53533

———

The Great River Road
If you can't travel the Mississippi by boat, you may as well explore it by automobile. The Great River Road highlights the communities along the greatest of American rivers. The route that is most relevant to the Black Hawk War would be the section from La Crosse, Wisconsin, to Rock Island, Illinois. The ten states along the Mississippi formed the River Parkway Commission (MRPC), which has been protecting historic sites and promoting tourism along the river since 1938.

This route is breathtakingly scenic and offers an off-the-beaten-path experience to leisurely explore the boating culture of the Midwest. Noted Black Hawk War sites along the river include Rock Island, Dubuque, Prairie du Chien and DeSoto, Wisconsin, near the Battle of Bad Axe.

———

Mississippi River Parkway Commission MRPC
701 East Washington Avenue, Suite 202
Madison, WI, 53703
experiencemississippiriver.com

———

Rock River Trail
A great blue heron flying over the Rock River is the logo that was adopted by the Rock River Trail. The in-depth tourist information provided by the nonprofit group makes for an ideal and leisurely option to exploring the area. Many of the communities along the Rock River contribute content to the endeavor and provide diverse options to explore the 320-mile trail from Rock Island, Illinois, to Fond du Lac, Wisconsin. Travelers are encouraged to display their accomplishment of traveling the route by purchasing their official Rock River Trail patch.

Rock River Visitors' Center
306 Dickop Street
South Beloit, IL, 61080
rockrivertrail.com

———

Glacial Heritage Trail

A series of interconnected "wheels and spokes" are the beginnings of a hoped-for systematic and convenient bike path and canoe access area that links together county, state and city parks in Jefferson, Rock and Walworth Counties in Wisconsin. The current bike trails often verge onto two-lane county roads, but the website details new developments and frequent community events in the area.

glacialheritagearea.org

———

Lincoln Highway, Route 66 and 30: From Chicago, Illinois, to Tama, Iowa

A latitude-inclined visitor may be interested in following the old Lincoln Highway from Chicago to Tama, Iowa, and the home of the Meskwaki Settlement. The route of the first national highway, the Lincoln Highway, provides a rather straight path that intersects with a number of worthwhile sites, as well as features sporadic references to the historic highway. Starting at the middle of the Macropolitan Region that Chicago is the heart of, you can depart from the site of the former Fort Dearborn, which was located about at the intersection of Michigan Avenue and Dearborn Avenue.

The active Lincoln Highway Association provides a breakdown of suggested highways that align with the original Route 66. For travelers looking to take the scenic route, stay on Route 30 and you'll wind your way through a number of downtowns. If that path becomes laborious, the parallel Route 80 can be used to streamline your travel time.

Notable sites from the Black Hawk War will include stops in Dixon, Illinois; the Quad Cities, including Rock Island; and historic Saukenuk, as well as Prophetstown and Shabbona, Illinois. This Chicago–Tama portion is just a fragment of the intercontinental highway that begins in New York and ends in San Francisco.

lincolnhighwayassoc.org

———

Ice Age Trail Alliance

Modeled after the great public treks on America's East Coast like the Appalachian Trail and the Long Trail, Wisconsin's Ice Age Trail invites the public to get outside and explore the natural environment. Contained entirely in Wisconsin, the trail ranges from Potawatomi State Park in Door County south toward the Illinois border and then north to Interstate State Park in St. Croix Falls. The 1,200 Visionary Trail is a work in progress, but communities along the passage continue to add to and improve segments.

For the Black Hawk War, the section of the Ice Age Trail that most closely aligns is from about Milton to Janesville. The routes includes Storrs Lake, a wooded section where Abe Lincoln camped, and then around Janesville, where the trail hugs the Rock River.

iceagetrail.org

SAUKENUK AND ROCK ISLAND

*We were friendly treated by the white chiefs....We found that troops had arrived
to build a fort at Rock Island [1816]. This in our opinion, was a contradiction
to what we had done [agreed to]. We did not, however, object to their building
the fort on the island, but we were very sorry, as this was the best island on the
Mississippi, and had long been the resort of our young people during the summer.
It was our garden which supplied us with strawberries, blackberries, gooseberries,
plums, apples and nuts of different kinds; and its waters supplied us with fine fish.
A good spirit had care of it, who lived in a cave in the rocks immediately under the
place where the fort now stands, and has often been seen by our people. He was
white, with large wings like a swan's, but ten times larger. But the noise of the fort
has since driven him away, and no doubt a bad spirit has taken his place!*
—Life of Black Hawk, *1833*

*The Sauk and Mesquaki tribes, usually spoken of as the Sauk and Fox, formed
a united nation. They had three villages about the vicinity of the mouth of Rock
River. One of these, a Fox village, was on the west side of the Mississippi where
Davenport, Iowa, now stands. The other two, both on the Illinois side, joined
at the edges. The one, a Fox village, was located opposite the lower end of Rock
Island, where the down-town part of the City of Rock Island now stands, and
the other was the Sauk village which adjoined it to the south and extended to the
bluff overlooking the Rock River, known as Black Hawk's Watch Tower.*
—Indian Trails Centering at Black Hawk's Village, *by John H.
Hauberg (1869–1955)*

T he woman spoke. Her name was not recorded in the official minutes of the meeting, but in 1831, she met with the American commander, General Gaines, at Fort Armstrong. Black Hawk related in his autobiography that she was the daughter of Ma-ta-tas, the old chief of Saukenuk. She had always been a friend of the whites and had even been wounded in fighting for them. The daughter of Ma-ta-tas spoke to General Gaines, with a staff in hand, and noted that her father would have told their people if the Saukenuk and their lands had been sold and that she had known the signers of the 1804 treaty. She was positive that they had never agreed to sell the land. She pleaded to remain with their fields and the burying ground of their ancestors.

General Gaines was not moved. The 1804 treaty was not changeable.

The official government minutes noted that Gaines stated the land now belonged to the Americans and the Sauk and Fox people must "move in three days, or they would be forced across the river." Gaines had brought with him from St. Louis a sizeable force of regular U.S. military, close to 1,400 troops and two warships. Disappointed and impressed with the size and firepower of General Gaines's troops, Black Hawk and his followers departed Saukenuk and crossed to the western shore of the Mississippi. The

Rock Island, United States Garrison, George Catlin, 1835–36. *Smithsonian American Art Museum, Gift of Mrs. Joseph Harrison Jr., object no. 1985.66.328.*

Sauk and Fox left their homeland, but the matter was not resolved. The unfairness of the situation simmered with Black Hawk.

Black Hawk related in his autobiography that in the spring of 1832, much of the tribe had reconciled with Keokuk's decision to remove the community from Saukenuk. Unfortunately, the people found difficult conditions in their new lands. The unbroken soil was not as fertile as the cropland they had nurtured over generations. The hunting and fishing was also poor. Black Hawk continued his political machinations by sending out messengers to regional tribes, including as far away as Arkansas and Texas.

By early spring in 1832, Black Hawk was resolved to try again, noting in his autobiography, "I had one consolation—for all the women were on my side, on account of their corn-fields." He had received news from Neopope that Wabokiesheik, also known as White Cloud or the Prophet, had promised support from the British and other First Nations to fight against the Americans. This included guns, ammunition, provisions, clothing and the assistance of the "nations on the lakes—Ottowas, Chippewas, Pottowatomies; and for the Winnebagos, he has them all at this command."

This misinformation, whether it was directly from the Prophet or Neopope, was not enough to move Keokuk. Black Hawk noted that after sharing the news with Keokuk, the latter called the messengers "liars" and said they should "remain where I was and keep quiet."

However, the hopeful news set Black Hawk in motion. He noted in his autobiography, "[C]onceiving that the peaceable disposition of Ke-o-kuck and his people had been, in a great measure, the cause of our having been driven from our village, I ascribed their present feelings to the same cause; and immediately went to work to recruit all my own band, and made preparations to ascend Rock River."

Black Hawk's British Band once again crossed the Mississippi River in the spring and made their way north. Instead of lingering in Saukenuk or Rock Island, they continued east up the Rock River to Prophetstown.

Gaines had been replaced by General Henry Atkinson, who did not immediately demonstrate a large show of force, as Gaines had done in 1831, according to an editorial in the May 2, 1832 *Galenian*:

We are informed by a correspondent at Rock Island, whose knowledge of the movement of the Indians is gained from personal observations, that this mischief has been long meditated by that [trio] of Indian Chiefs. They have been sending wampum to several Indian nations for the purpose of

Modern reconstruction of Fort Armstrong on Arsenal Island.

enlisting them to take part in their nefarious cause. They say, too, that many will aid them, and that they are promised succor from the British—that they expect their ammunition, etc., from the British. They have not consented to listen to the counsels of any Indians who are friendly to the U. States.

Sites and Museums Near the Quad Cities

The Mississippi River takes a break from its southerly flow, and for a stretch, it travels almost directly due west. Along this straightening is a series of islands. Black Hawk noted the spiritual importance that the island held for his people. Rock Island, now called Arsenal Island, has been the location of the Rock Island Arsenal since the 1850s. The facility has been the muscle of America's military, supplying the ordnance and ammunition for wars since the Civil War.

Due south from Arsenal Island is the city of Rock Island, which isn't an "island" but rather retains the name of the island that was instrumental in its development. The area today is well known as the Quad Cities, which consists of Davenport and Bettendorf, Iowa, on the west side of the Mississippi and Rock Island and East Moline, Illinois, on the east side.

Rock Island Arsenal

The Rock Island Arsenal is an operating military base that requires guests to pre-register and undergo a background check. If you receive a "favorable criminal background check before entry," you are welcome to visit the facility. If you are unsure if you would receive a favorable response, you should perhaps take this venue off of your itinerary. The wait to clear the entry gate is similar to grabbing a flight out of a medium-size airport, but with a waiting room that feels akin to that of the Department of Motor Vehicles. Once on the island, visitors must stay on designated guest roadways.

The museum includes information on the Sauk and Fox settlement on Rock Island, as well as a desk that likely was used for signing the 1832 Treaty with the Sac and Fox Nations. The main focus of the museum is the armaments and production history of the island. The bulk of the exhibit focuses on guns, armaments and more produced at the military factory on the island.

The Arsenal Historical Society
1 Rock Island Arsenal
Building 60, 3500 North Avenue
Rock Island, IL, 61299-5000
arsenalhistoricalsociety.org

GEORGE DAVENPORT HOUSE
The home built by George Davenport in 1833–34 is one of the oldest structures in the area. The home is within the gates of the Rock Island Arsenal, so guests need to follow the background check procedures at the main entrance of the armory to access the site. The attraction is open from May to October for a small free. Contact the foundation for upcoming events and special tours.

COLONEL DAVENPORT HISTORICAL FOUNDATION
May–October, Wednesday–Saturday, from 12:00 p.m. to 4:00 p.m.
P.O. Box 4603
Rock Island, IL, 61204-4603
(309) 786-7336
coloneldavenport1833@hotmail.com

———

JOHN HAUBERG INDIAN MUSEUM
This collection of Native American and frontier history is assembled in a stately brick building erected by the Civilian Conservation Corps. The exhibits include Black Hawk's plaster life mask, as well as perhaps the largest accessible collection of Native American artifacts relating to the Sauk and Fox Nations.

The building is set on a majestic overlook with striking views of the Mississippi River Valley. The local tradition holds that Black Hawk was in the habit of climbing a towering cottonwood tree on the bluff in order to survey the valley. A series of "Black Hawk Towers" built on this hill served as community recreation and gathering places. This includes venues for dining, toboggan runs down the hillside and areas for grand performances. During the centennial of the construction of Fort Armstrong in 1916, the community of Rock Island held a series of fanciful pageants and exhibitions. These included inviting members of the Sauk and Fox Nations from Iowa and Oklahoma.

John Henry Hauberg (1869–1955) of Rock Island was an enthusiastic proponent of preserving and celebrating the Sauk and Fox traditions. His collection of artifacts and historic items are the foundation for the exhibits at the Black Hawk State Historic Site. Hauberg led the effort to petition the Illinois state legislature for the construction of the current building erected in 1937.

Statue of Black Hawk outside the Black Hawk State Historic Site, Rock Island, Illinois.

Hauberg was also instrumental in building relationships with the Meskwaki Settlement and the Sac and Fox Nations in Oklahoma and Kansas. This includes inviting the tribe to hold a powwow in 1940 that became an annual event for many years.

Outside the museum resides a Black Hawk statue that once stood in Spencer Square. The *Rock Island Argus* reported on November 28, 1892, on the unveiling of this statue, donated by O.J. Dimick. The festivities included Bleuer's band performing "patriotic airs" along with a pyrotechnic exhibit. It was hoped that the statue would be erected close to the corner of Twelfth and Ninth Streets, which, according to local tradition was the center of Saukenuk.

1510 Forty-Sixth Avenue
Rock Island, Illinois
(309) 788-9536
blackhawkpark.org

———

Fort Armstrong
When traveling on Fort Armstrong Road over Arsenal Island, motorists have a brief opportunity to pull over and visit a memorial and small reconstruction of Fort Armstrong. This site is outside the Rock Island Armory grounds, so visitors don't need to go through the registration required to get onto the base. The reconstruction is rather modest; however, the view is pleasant, and lucky tourists may glimpse a majestic white pelican.

Fort Armstrong Road
Rock Island, IL, 61201

———

Black Hawk Mural, Rock Island, Illinois
Richard Haas (born in 1936) grew up in Wisconsin in rural Plain, outside Spring Green. He would become instrumental in developing the national movement of large-scale outdoor public murals. His pieces often involve "trompe l'oeil," which creates the illusion of depth and a three-dimensional effect on two-dimensional surfaces. Haas's first mural to incorporate Black Hawk's image was produced in 1985 on the former Olin Park overlook near the capitol building in Madison, Wisconsin. The mural was painted on a retaining wall and imagined an aspirational public center envisioned by Frank Lloyd Wright. Ironically, the City of Madison did finally decide to build the convention center "inspired" by Frank Lloyd Wright on that site in 1997. The Monona Terrace Convention Center now obscures the Haas mural. The panel of Black Hawk looking out onto the lake is hidden from view. Now Black Hawk watches over the building's parking garage and four lanes of traffic on John Nolen Drive.

Haas would return to Black Hawk as the focus for his monumental work in Rock Island, Illinois, in 1993. The mural is modeled after the Black Hawk statue of 1892 that resides outside the John Hauberg Indian Museum. The mural depicts a sixty-foot-tall Black Hawk, seemingly jutting out of the building as a three-dimensional sculpture.

1701 Second Avenue
Rock Island, IL, 61201

A WHITE FLAG AND THE CONFLICT BEGINS

This monument shall stand, as every day, no doubt, Black Hawk himself stood, in silent prayer to the Great Master at sunrise and sunset. So may this monument stand in silent prayer, proclaiming, to generations to come, that after all we are children of the same Maker, and we are all brothers.
—*Ohiyesa, member of the Sioux Nation, who addressed the unveiling of* The Eternal Indian, *the Black Hawk monument outside Oregon, Illinois, in 1911*

To him who died in exile, chieftain still,
A victim of our greed, with broken heart,
We raise this sentinel of the hill,
This splendid symbol of remorseful Art.
—*Hamlin Garland's "The Trail Makers," presented at the unveiling of* The Eternal Indian

In the weeks that followed Black Hawk's crossing of the Mississippi River, General Atkinson struggled to understand the motives of the British Band. He convened a gathering of Sauk and Fox chiefs who had agreed to depart from their lands east of the Mississippi. Keokuk stated that the Sauk and Fox wished to leave in peace on their new allotment of lands west of the Mississippi. Atkinson warned Keokuk not to communicate with the British Band and to stay away from their former lands.

The new Indian agent at Rock Island, Felix St. Vrain, met with the Prophet about the actions of the British Band. St. Vrain was incredulous when the Prophet told him that he had invited Black Hawk and his followers to live in his village on the Rock River. The Prophet noted that he saw no harm in inviting them to his village. St. Vrain asked the Prophet if he really expected the Americans to not force him and his people from his village. The Prophet replied, "I did not; perhaps you expect to do so, but you may lay my bones there."

The Prophet may have reasoned that since he was half Winnebago and half Sauk, and perhaps technically outside the formal treaties that each tribe had signed with the Americans, he was free to live as leader of the village of Prophetstown. He had no treaty with the Americans, limiting his territory.

The April 17 *Missouri Republican* printed a report from the "military expedition" under General Atkinson. Its sources noted that "the Prophet is the chief instigator of the present difficulties, and he is seconded in his nefarious schemes by Black Hawk. These two Indians, with their followers, are now on or near the spot whence Black Hawk was removed last summer." The account presumes that the group was bound for Canada via Chicago. The author noted that "they have no intention of striking the whites first—and this is about the amount of what we do know positively."

Atkinson sent intermediaries to Black Hawk on April 24. The correspondence chastises the British Bands' actions: "I advise you to come back and re-cross the Mississippi without delay. It is not too late to do what is right—and what is right do once. If you do not come back and go on the other side of the great river I shall write to your great father [President Jackson] and tell him of your bad conduct....Some foolish people have told you that the British will assist you—do not believe it—you will find when it is too late that it is not true."

The Sauk emissaries, W-ka-me and Pa-che-noi, responded a few days later with Black Hawk's reply. Atkinson received a joint response to his demands of the British Band. Neopope and Black Hawk noted that they had been "invited by the Winnebagoes at Peketolica to go and live with them." They had no "bad feelings" and had no "bad intentions." Black Hawk also noted, "I do not command the Indians. The Village belongs to the Chiefs. Why do they want to know my feelings. I have no bad feelings. My opinions goes with the Chief."

Atkinson was now forced to try and muster a display of force like General Gaines had successfully accomplished the year before. However, the British Band had already passed by Fort Armstrong and had ascended the Rock River past Prophetstown. Atkinson now was in the position of chasing the British Band to force a settlement.

The American forces arrived at Prophetstown prepared for a confrontation. But they found an empty, abandoned village. The U.S. Army burned the lodges in the village, sparking the first act of aggression in the conflict. The torching of the lodges and crops was hoped to send the clear message that the members of the British Band had no hope of remaining in their homes east of the Mississippi River.

The British Band and the Prophet's followers had all moved farther up the river by the time Atkinson's force arrived. While General Atkinson continued moving his regular, enlisted troops slowly up the Rock River, he allowed Major Isaiah Stillman and his Illinois militia to forge ahead. The Rock River posed an impediment for Atkinson's chain of supply. He noted that his boats were too large to navigate up the rapids and that he did not want to separate his regular troops from their equipment and food. Leaving the trained American forces behind, Stillman led his troops to Dixon's Ferry and across the Rock River.

As the British Band moved farther up the river, Black Hawk began to learn from his discussions with Potawatomi and Winnebago chiefs that the support from the British, as well as other First Nations, was not going to materialize. Black Hawk noted his autobiography that Keokuk's warnings had been true: "We had been deceived! All the fair promises through Neopope were false."

On April 28, John Dixon, the proprietor of the lodge and ferry at Dixon's Crossing, related to Major Isaiah Stillman the location and size of the British Band: more than five hundred horses, one hundred canoes and likely five hundred men. He added that they were not a threat and were "going to raise corn and build a town on the Pottawattimies land, whose line is within 12 miles of me on this side of the [Rock] River."

North of Dixon, the forces of Major Stillman and a handful of British Band members, under a flag of truce, met. Black Hawk related in his autobiography:

I had resolved upon giving up the war—and sent a flag of peace to the American war chief—expecting, as a matter of right, reason and justice, that our flag would be respected (I have always seen it so in war among the whites) and a council convened, that we might explain our grievances, having been driven from our village the year before, without being permitted to gather the corn and provisions which our women had labored hard to cultivate, and ask for permission to return—thereby giving up all idea of going to war against the whites. Yet, instead of this honorable course which I have always practiced in war, I was forced into WAR, with about five hundred warriors, to content against three or four thousand!

The undisciplined militia of Major Stillman fired on and killed members of the peace party. Andrew Maxfield, a volunteer in the militia, shared his experience in the battle in the *Sangamo Journal*:

> *After a pursuit of about five miles up Rock River, we overtook the fugitives, and found them armed with bows and arrows, spears and rifles....We recognized a red flag and ordered them to surrender. This order being disobeyed we fired and brought down three Indians and one poney. The Indians now rallied to the number of about 30, and moved towards us with moderation. We then fell back across the ravine till we were reinforced.... The Indians were now seen by the glimmering moon light, on three sides like swarms of summer insects. Our lines never again formed. Some companies formed and fired, and were thrown into confusion by the retreat of others.... Our camp then resounded as though five hundred men were under the torture of the tomahawk and scalping knife. I heard orders given by some man to "Kill those d----d Indian prisoners." It is true there was, perhaps, one case of inebriation. On our march about ten miles from Sycamore, it was found that the baggage wagon was too heavy. One barrel of whiskey was therefore, headed and all our canteens filled.*

Atkinson noted of the battle, "I regret that General Stillman was sent to reconnoiter the Indians before my arrival....It has not only encouraged the Indians but closed the door against settling the difficulty without bloodshed." The routing of about three hundred militia by a few dozen members of the British Band escalated the conflict and ended the opportunity for a peaceful resolution. In addition to the twelve militia members killed, the battle spread panic across the territory. Black Hawk related in his autobiography, "[N]ever was I so much surprised in this attack! An army of three or four hundred, after having learned that we were suing for peace, to attempt to kill the flag-bearers."

NORTHERN ILLINOIS AREA SITES AND MUSEUMS

STILLMAN'S DEFEAT MEMORIAL SITE

Near downtown Stillman, Illinois, a memorial was erected to honor the American militia members who were killed during the battle. Because the fighting took place over a widespread area, the fallen were first interred in individual graves but were later moved and honored in this central monument on June 13, 1902. The fifty-foot-high pillar has four granite engraved plaques at its base. The names of each of the American fallen are inscribed, as is the following: "In memory of the Illinois volunteers who fell at Stillman's Run, May 15, 1832. The presence of the Soldier, Statesman, Martyr Abraham Lincoln assisting in the burial of these honored dead has made this spot more sacred."

225 Spruce Street (corner of Spruce and East Roosevelt Streets, Highway 72) Stillman Valley, IL, 61084

————

PROPHETSTOWN
Small plaque noting the general area of the historic Native American community of Prophetstown, at the intersection of Star Road and Johnson Drive.

————

NORTHWEST TERRITORY HISTORIC CENTER
A regional historic museum that focuses on exhibits, dioramas and information on the American frontier and early farming history. It includes sections on Native American history and the Black Hawk War. There is a small entrance fee.

205 West Fifth Street
Dixon, IL, 61021
nthc.org

————

LINCOLN STATUE *THE CAPTAIN* AND DIXON'S CABIN
Dixon's Ferry was a key crossing on the Rock River. A re-creation of John Dixon's cabin and a statue of Lincoln in his militia garb entitled *The Captain* by Leonard Crunelle was dedicated on August 23, 1930.

Lincoln Statue Drive and North Hennepin Avenue
Dixon, IL, 61021

ABRAHAM LINCOLN'S SERVICE
IN THE BLACK HAWK WAR

The Bear Hunt
But who did this, and how to trace
What's true from what's a lie,
like lawyers, in a murder case
they stoutly argufy.
—*Abraham Lincoln, 1846*

braham Lincoln's public written record begins in 1832. Weeks before the
onset of the Black Hawk War, a young Lincoln submitted a letter to the
local newspaper, the *Sangamon Journal*. In the centerfold of the four-page
issue of the weekly paper, Lincoln introduces himself to his community as
a candidate for Illinois State Assembly. His first public thoughts belie the
characteristics of the understated and uniquely laborious writing style that
he would hone and perfect during his political career. His focus on local
issues, and the step-by-step logical process in his determination of turning
the shallow Sangamon River into a source of commerce, is reprinted in full
here. The entire collection of the *Sangamon* newspaper has been digitized by
the University of Illinois–Urbana and provides a worthwhile overview of
the news of the day.

To the People of Sangamon County

FELLOW CITIZENS: *Having become a candidate for the honorable office*
of one of your representatives in the next General Assembly of this state,

in accordance with an established custom, and the principles of true republicanism, it becomes my duty to make known to you—the people whom I propose to represent—my sentiments with regard to local affairs.

Time and experience have verified a demonstration, the public utility of internal improvements. That the poorest and most thinly populated countries would be greatly benefitted by the opening of good roads, and in the clearing of navigable streams within their limits, is what no person will deny. But yet it is folly to undertake works of this or any other kind, without first knowing that we are able to finish them—as half finished work generally proves to be labor lost. There cannot justly be any objection to having rail roads and canals, any more than to other good things, provided they cost nothing. The only objection is to paying for them; and the objection to paying arises from the want of ability to pay.

With respect to the county of Sangamon, some more easy means of communication than we now possess, for the purpose of facilitating the take of exporting the surplus products of its fertile soil, and importing necessary articles from abroad, are indispensable necessary. A meeting has been held of the citizens of Jacksonville, and the adjacent country, for the purpose of deliberating and enquiring into the expediency of constructing a rail road from some eligible point on the Illinois river, through the town of Jacksonville, in Morgan county, to the town of Springfield, in Sangamon county. This is, indeed, a very desirable object. No other improvement that reason will justify us in hoping for, can equal in utility the rail road. It is a never failing source of communication, between places of business remotely situated from each other. Upon the rail road the regular progress of commercial intercourse is not interrupted by either high or low water, or freezing weather, which are the principal difficulties that render our future hopes of water communication precarious and uncertain. Yet, however desirable an object the construction of a rail road through our country may be; however high our imaginations may be heated at thoughts of it—there is always a heart appalling shock accompanying the account of its cost, which forces us to shrink from our pleasing anticipation. The probable cost of this contemplated rail road is estimated at $290,000;—the bare statement of which, in my opinion, is sufficient to justify the belief, that the improvement of Sangamo river is an object much better suited to our infant resources.

Respecting this view, I think I may say, without the fear of being contradicted, that its navigation may be rendered completely practicable, as high as the mouth of the South Fork, or probably higher, to vessels of from 25 to 30 tons burthen, for at least one half of all common years, and

SURVEYOR'S NOTICE,
I HAVE appointed John B. Watson, Abram
Lincoln and John Calhoun Deputy Survey-
ors for Sangamon County. In my absence
from town any persons wishing their lands surveyed, will do well to call at the Recorder's
office and enter his or their names in a book
left for that purpose, stating the township and
range in which they respectively live, and their
business shall be promptly attended to.
Sept. 10, 1835.   T. M. NEALE.

Notice of Abraham Lincoln as a
surveyor, *Sangamon Journal*, 1835.

*to vessels of much greater burthen a part of that time. From my peculiar
circumstances, it is probable that for the last twelve months I have given
as particular attention to the state of the water in this river, as any other
person in the country. In the month of March, 1831, in company with
others, I commenced the building of a flat boat on the Sangamon, and
finished and took her out in the course of the spring. Since that time, I
have been concerned in the mill at New Salem. These circumstances are
sufficient evidence, that I have not been very inattentive to the stages of
the water. The time at which we crossed the mill dam, being in the last
days of April, the water was lower than it had been since the breaking of
winter in February, or than it was for several weeks after. The principal
difficulties we encountered in descending the river, were from the drifted
timber, which obstructions all know is not difficult to be removed. Knowing
almost precisely the height of water at the time, I believe I am safe in saying
that it has as often been higher as lower since.*

*From this view of the subject, it appears that my calculations with
regard to the navigation of the Sangamo, cannot be unfounded in reason;
but whatever may be its natural advantages, certain it is, that it never can
be practically useful to any great extent, without being greatly improved by
art. The drifted timber, as I have before mentioned, is the most formidable
barrier to this object. Of all parts of this river, none will require so much
labor in proportion, to make it navigable, as the last thirty or thirty-five
miles; and going with the meanderings of the channel, when we are this
distance above its mouth, we are only between twelve and eighteen miles
above Beardstown, in something near a straight direction; and this route is
upon such low ground as to retain water in many places during the season,
and in all parts such as to draw two-thirds or three-fourths of the river
water at all high stages.*

*This route is upon prairie land the whole distance;—so that it appears
to me, by removing the turf, a sufficient width and damming up the old
channel, the whole river in a short time would wash its way through,
thereby curtailing the distance, and increasing the velocity of the current*

very considerably, while there would be no timber upon the banks to obstruct its navigation in future; and being nearly straight, the timber which might float in at the head, would be apt to go clear through. There are also many places above this where the river, in its zig zag course, forms such complete peninsulas, as to be easier cut through at the necks than to remove the obstructions from the bends—which if done, would also lessen the distance.

What the cost of this work would be, I am unable to say. It is probable, however, it would not be greater than is common to streams of the same length. Finally, I believe the improvement of the Sangamon river, to be vastly important and highly desireable to the people of this country; and if elected, any measure in the legislature having this for its object, which may appear judicious, will meet my approbation, and shall receive my support.

It appears the practice of loaning money at exorbitant rates of interest, has already been opened as a field for discussion; so I suppose I may enter upon it without claiming the honor, or risking the danger, which may await its first explorer. It seems as though we are never to have an end to this baneful and corroding system, acting almost as prejudicial to the general interests of the community as a direct tax of several thousand dollars annually laid on each county, for the benefit of a few individuals only, unless there be a law made setting a limit to the rates of usury. A law for this purpose, I am of opinion, may be made, without materially injuring any class of people. In cases of extreme necessity there could always be means found to cheat the law, while in all other cases it would have its intended effect. I would not favor the passage of a law upon this subject, which might be very easily evaded. Let it be such that the labor and difficulty of evading it, could only be justified in cases of the greatest necessity.

Upon the subject of education, not presuming to distaste any plan or system respecting it, I can only say that I view it as the most important subject which we as a people can be engaged in. That every man may receive at least, a moderate education, and thereby be enabled to read the histories of his own and other countries, by which he may duly appreciate the value of our free institutions, appears to be an object of vital importance, even on this account alone, to say nothing of the advantages and satisfaction to be derived from all being able to read the scriptures and other works, both of a religious and moral nature, for themselves. For my part, I desire to see the time when education, and by its means, morality, sobriety, enterprise and industry, shall become much more general than at present, and should be gratified to have it in my power to contribute something to the advancement of any measure which might have a tendency to accelerate the happy period.

With regard to existing laws, some alterations are thought to be necessary. Many respectable men have suggested that our estray [sic] laws—respecting the issuing of executions, the road law, and some others, are deficient in their present form, and require alterations. But considering the great probability that the framers of those laws were wiser than myself, I should prefer not meddling with them, unless they were first attacked by others, in which case I should feel it both a privilege and a duty to take that stand, which in my view, might tend most to the advancement of justice.

But, Fellow-Citizens, I shall conclude. Considering the great degree of modesty which should always attend youth, it is probable I have already been more presuming than becomes me. However, upon the subjects of which I have treated, I have spoken as I thought. I may be wrong in regard to any or all of them; but holding it a sound maxim, that it is better to be only sometimes right, than at all times wrong, so soon as I discover my opinions to be erroneous, I shall be ready to renounce them.

Every man is said to have his peculiar ambition. Whether it be true or not, I can say for one that I have no other so great as that of being truly esteemed of my fellow men, by rendering myself worthy of their esteem. How far I shall succeed in gratifying this ambition, is yet to be developed. I am young and unknown to many of you. I was born and have ever remained in the most humble walks of life. I have not wealthy or popular relations to recommend me. My case is thrown exclusively upon the independent voters of this country, and if elected they will have conferred a favor upon me, for which I shall be unremitting in my labors to compensate. But if the good people in their wisdom shall see fit to keep me in the background, I have been too familiar with disappointments to be very much chagrined.

Your friend and fellow-citizen, ABRAHAM LINCOLN. New Salem, March 9, 1832.

It may strike citizens today as rather amazing that a prospective elected official would have the temerity to break down such a comprehensive campaign statement. Not only is the length of Lincoln's letter many times the common political statement of today, but it also lacks the superfluous, self-congratulatory language of modern political speeches. This is a bare-bones and reasoned argument that also breaks down Lincoln's thought process point by point. The topics of his focus—economic development by expanding the utility of the Sangamon River and expanding railroad access, limiting usurious interest rates, education and editing current

Black Hawk illustration. *From* History of the Indian Wars, *by Henry Trumbull (1846).*

laws—provide a snapshot into key issues facing his frontier community. The length of the letter is also much longer than present-day newspapers would accept. In 2020, Springfield, Illinois's local paper, the *State Journal-Register*, has a policy of only printing the first 250 words of a letter to the editors. Lincoln's letter of more than 8,400 words would likely be rejected or edited into oblivion by an editor today. In the era of Twitter, Lincoln's letter would span thirty tweets.

The Sangamon River would never become an acceptable waterway for the transportation of goods or people. In fact, within a few years after the Black Hawk War, the community would be dispersed and the buildings abandoned. If not for the brief residency of Abraham Lincoln, the frontier settlement of New Salem, in Sangamon County, Illinois, would have been forgotten.

Today, the town of New Salem lives again, with reenactors dressed in 1830s distressed burlap clothing, milling about and partaking in blacksmithing, sweeping pine board cabins, keeping wood-burning stoves stoked and elucidating for tourists on the hardships and joys experienced by the first citizens of the state of Illinois. Visitors to the area today may be struck by the low course the Sangamon River displays as it winds its way through the county on its journey to the Mississippi.

The reconstructed settlement has faithfully utilized archaeological research to approximate the size and layout of the pioneer town that Lincoln dreamed of becoming a river city. While only one of the actual buildings is extant from the town, the attraction provides a well-designed homage to Lincoln's frontier life.

From April 7, 1832, to early July, Lincoln would serve as a volunteer militiaman. While his contingent never came into contact with hostile forces, he did experience a series of rapid, forced marches and weeks of brutal conditions in the wilderness.

Lincoln's law partner, William Herndon (1818–1891), compiled a biography, *Herndon's Lincoln: The True Story of a Great Life*. The main theme of Herndon's recollections of Abe's Black Hawk stories was the uncomfortable living conditions, the "ruffian" character of his fellow soldiers and the lack of food. At Turtle Village—near present-day Beloit, Wisconsin—Lincoln and his company availed themselves of the chickens and remnants left at the cabin of a squatter who had abandoned the homestead. Even though the conditions were unpleasant, Lincoln did volunteer for a second tour. Herndon doesn't detail any of Lincoln's comments on being near the main conflict or the aftermath of Stillman's Run.

Herndon wrote that while many biographies of the time noted Lincoln's patriotism as the primary reason for enlisting in the Black Hawk War, Lincoln himself had noted to Herndon, "I was out of work and there being no danger of more fighting, I could do nothing better than enlist again."

In the Life of Jefferson Davis, a biography written by Jefferson Davis's wife after the former Confederate president had passed away, asserts that Davis himself took Lincoln's oath of service. Her recollection of the austere and dashing Davis meeting the "tall, gawky, homely young man" of Lincoln is purely fanciful. Davis was on leave during Lincoln's enlistment in the conflict.

Since Lincoln's tragic death, his every movement across the continent has been festooned with plaques and commemorations. Across Northern Illinois, travelers today will find statues, monuments and historic markers noting his series of debates with Stephen Douglas in 1858. What is striking is the dearth of writing Lincoln left us in on his opinions and experiences during his service in the Black Hawk War. While modern politicians who have served in the military will proudly (and often) tout their service, Lincoln's militia service does not play a role in much of Lincoln's speeches or writing. While he witnessed a dramatic sea change in the explosive growth of

Michael Mayosky's mural of a young Abraham Lincoln as a surveyor. Springfield, Illinois.

American settlement as the frontier paths he walked were transformed into roads and railroads and makeshift cabins were replaced with brick buildings along surveyed city grids, he didn't provide many details or references to his military service in his writings or public speeches.

In 1850, Benjamin Drake published *The Life and Adventures of Black Hawk: With Sketches of Keokuk, the Sac and Fox Indians and the late Black Hawk War.* A copy of this publication once owned by a militiaman in the conflict, Abraham Lincoln, resides at the Illinois Historical Society. The book is on display at the Lincoln Home National Historic Site and would have been in Lincoln's library in Springfield from about 1850 to 1861. The fact that he owned a copy of this book may demonstrate that Lincoln had at least a passing interest in the historian's account of the conflict.

Perhaps Drake's words in the opening preface of the account of the war weighed on Lincoln's decision not to highlight his service later in his political career. In the foreword of Drake's text, the historian questions the motives and fairness of the conflict, as well as America's policies in dealing with American Indians:

We gravely recognize them [American Indians] as an independent people, and treat them as vassals: We make solumn compacts with them, which we interpret as our interest dictates, but punish them, if they follow the example: We admit their title to the land which they occupy, and at the same time literally compel them to sell it to us upon our own terms: We send agents and missionaries to reclaim them from the error of their ways—to bring them from the hunter to the pastoral life; and yet permit our citizens to debase them by spirituous liquors, and cheat them out of their property: We make war upon them without any adequate cause—pursue them without mercy—and put them to death, without regard to age, sex, or condition: And, then deliberately proclaim to the world that they are savages—cruel and untameable—degraded and faithless.

On July 16, 1832, young Abraham Lincoln and his cohort George Harrison, along with scores of other Illinois militia, were honorably relieved of their service in the Black Hawk War. A wooden sign outside the village of Cold Spring, on a knoll named "Lincoln's Hill," notes the spot where Abe's horse was stolen from him the day after he concluded his second term of service, as tradition holds.

As Abe and George began their way back down the Rock River to Illinois, the future president missed the opportunity to meet General Scott. The already battle-wearied military leader would later be known by the moniker "Old Fuss and Feathers." Some thirty years later, at the outset of the Civil War, Lincoln would rely on Scott's military mind in the early dealings of the conflict.

In late 1859, Lincoln would write a remembrance of his service in the Illinois militia. He wrote a short autobiography for Jesse W. Fell to use as a basis for a more formal political biography for Lincoln's campaign. Lincoln noted that his grandfather Abraham Lincoln was waylaid and killed by Indians in 1781 or 1782. Lincoln detailed his hardscrabble upbringing, in which he was "raised to farm work" until the age of twenty-two, when in Sangamon he became "sort of a Clerk in a store" until he signed up for service in the Black Hawk War. He noted, "I was elected Captain of Volunteers—a success which gave me more pleasure than any I have had since." Lincoln mentioning being elected as a captain as a great honor and then not describing that moment, or indeed his ensuing serving in that role, is perplexing.

In Milwaukee on September 39, 1859, Lincoln would return to the general area in which he served in the Illinois Militia. He addressed the luminaries at the Wisconsin State Agricultural Society in Milwaukee, whereupon he extolled the values of farmers, agriculture and the "young, prosperous, and soon to be, great State of Wisconsin." Lincoln then, in a similar fashion as his inaugural writing in the *Sangamon Journal* in 1832, laid out an impassioned and logical treatise on the importance of cultivation, combining labor and education and the principle of thorough work.

Lincoln, however, did not take this occasion to reflect more on his direct connection to the Northwest Territory—now Wisconsin—and relate the exponential growth of American civilization, or even share a story of his travails camping in the wilds. This omission is frustrating to the modern ambulator. Perhaps the humility of Lincoln's personality kept him for enmeshing his own personal story into the more important matter at hand of building the agricultural industry.

Following his address in Milwaukee, Lincoln traveled to Janesville and spoke to the citizens of that growing city on the shores of the Rock River. When Lincoln first traveled through the area in 1832, it was an unpopulated prairie and oak savannah with an occasional American Indian village. The native trails he had walked on were now serving as foundations for wagon trails, roads, railroads and crossroads for continued American settlement. The building he spoke at in 1859 in Janesville is now a parking lot that overlooks a massive mural of Black Hawk and a white buffalo, with mountain peaks in the background.

The most oft-cited reference to Lincoln's time in the 1832 conflict came during his time in the U.S. House of Representatives. It is striking that he used the Black Hawk War as an example not to elevate his own wartime service but to humorously diminish his military service. He downplayed his services to lightly attack Lewis Cass, the presidential candidate running against Lincoln's chosen candidate, Zachary Taylor. Lincoln may have been aware that in the balance of American conflicts, his didn't measure up to many who served during more dangerous battles. Lincoln's scant reference to his service in the militia came during his time serving as a U.S. Representative from Illinois. On July 27, 1848, he delivered a speech on the "Presidential Question," in which he defended the record of his party's candidate, General Taylor, and attempted to undermine the other candidate, General Cass of Michigan.

Near the end of the speech, available in *Abraham Lincoln: Speeches and Writings, 1832–1858*, Lincoln derided Cass's military service in a section dubbed "Military Trail of the Great Michigander." Lincoln scolded the other party for its attempts to build General Cass up as a grand military commander:

He [General Cass] *was not at Hull's surrender, but he was close by; he was volunteer to General Harrison on the day of the battle of the Thames; and, as you said in 1840, Harrison was picking huckleberries two miles off while the battle was fought, I suppose it is a just conclusion with you, to say Cass was aiding Harrison to pick huckleberries. This is about all, except the mooted question of the broken sword. Some authors say he broke it, some say he threw it away, and some others, who ought to know, say nothing about it. Perhaps it would be a fair historical compromise to say, if he did not break it, he didn't do anything else with it.*

By the way, Mr. Speaker, did you know I am a military hero? Yes, sir; in the days of the Black Hawk war, I fought, bled, and came away. Speaking of General Cass' career, reminds me of my own. I was not at Stillman's defeat, but I was about as near it, as Cass was to Hulls surrender; and, like him, I saw the place very soon afterwards. It is quite certain I did not break my sword, for I had none to break; but I bent a musket pretty badly on one occasion. If Cass broke his sword, the idea is, he broke it in desperation; I bent the musket by accident. If General Cass went in advance of me in picking huckleberries, I guess I surpassed him in charges upon the wild onions. If he saw any live, fighting Indians, it was more than I did; but I had a good many bloody struggles with the musquetoes; and, although I never fainted from the loss of blood, I can truly say I was often hungry. Mr. Speaker, if I should ever conclude to doff whatever our democratic friends may suppose there is of black cockade federalism about me, and thereupon, they shall take me up as their candidate for Presidency, I protest they shall not make fun of me, as they have of General Cass, by attempting to write me into a military hero.

One can imagine the local historians in the 1890s of Stillman, Illinois, deciding against quoting directly from Lincoln as they planned out their memorial to consecrate the burial site of soldiers killed during Stillman's Run. Engraving into stone Lincoln's words "I saw the place very soon afterwards" doesn't have quite the same noble ring to it as their chosen language: "The presence of the Soldier, Statesman, Martyr Abraham Lincoln assisting in the burial of these honored dead has made this spot more sacred."

After belittling Cass's military service, Lincoln referred to and minimized his own service as a rhetorical strategy to insulate Cass from returning the criticism. Lincoln in essence undermined any response Cass might have after Lincoln delivered this address.

There are a number of thirdhand and fuzzily remembered stories of Lincoln by other participants in the Illinois Militia. Accounts include a young

Abe standing up to fellow militia members to spare the life of an elderly tribal member who was left behind by the main contingent of the British Band.

The most telling firsthand account of Lincoln's time in the militia comes from a letter of one of his fellow service members. In *An Oral History of Abraham Lincoln: John G. Nicolay's Interviews and Essays*, edited by Michael Burlingame, a letter written years after the war by George Harrison to the newly elected Lincoln in May 1860 displays a clear snapshot of Lincoln's role in the conflict:

May 29, 1860

Respected Sir:

In view of the intimacy that at one time subsisted between yourself and me, I deem it my duty as well as privilege, now that the intensity of the excitement of recent transactions is a little passed from you and from me, after the crowd of congratulations already received from many friends, also to offer you my heartfelt congratulations on your very exalted position in our great Republican party. No doubt but that you will become tired of the flattery of cringing, selfish adulators. But I think you will know that way [what] *I say I feel.*

For the attachment commenced in the Black Hawk campaign while we messed together with Johnson, Fancher, and Wyatt, when we ground our coffee in the same tin cup with the hatchett handle—baked our bread on our ramrods around the same fire—ate our fried meat off the same piece of elm bark—slept in the same tent every night—traveled together by day and by night in search of the savage foe—and together scoured the tall grass on the battle ground of the skirmish near Gratiot's Grove in search of the slain— with very many incidents too tedious to name—and consummated on our afoot and canoe journey home, must render us incapable of deception.

Since the time mentioned, our pursuits have called me to operate a little apart; yours, as you formerly hinted, to a course of political and legal struggle; mine to agriculture and medicine. The success that we have both enjoyed, I am happy to know, is very encouraging. I am also glad to know, although we must act in vastly different spheres, that we are enlisted for the promotion of the same great cause: the cause which, next to revealed religion (which is humility and love) is most dear: the cause of Liberty, as set forth by true republicanism and not rank abolitionism.

Then let us go on in the discharge of duty, trusting, for aid, to the Great Universal Ruler.

Yours truly,
George M. Harrison

This remembrance by Harrison provides the most accessible firsthand description of Lincoln's life as a militia member. George Harrison and Abraham traveled by canoe and on foot back to their homes from present-day Cold Spring, Wisconsin, to Sangamon County, Illinois. While their role in the conflict was complete, General Atkinson still had at this command a potent force in the field to confront the elusive British Band.

Years later, Lincoln would support the candidacy of his fellow Black Hawk War veteran and Whig Party member General Zachary Taylor in the 1848 election. The presidential biography of Taylor highlighted his prolific military service, including his role in the Black Hawk War. While Taylor had a forty-year-long military career, the Kentucky native openly and positively described his service during the Black Hawk War. His biography notes his service in the Northwest, where from 1826 to 1836 he served and helped to bring an end to the Black Hawk War, an "affair that may be summarily expressed as a charge of regulars, and of Dodge's Rangers, a retreat and a rout."

President Taylor would end up serving only a brief sixteen months in office, succumbing to a sickness that may have been cholera. Upon Taylor's passing, Abraham Lincoln was chosen to memorialize the passing of the president, "Old Rough and Ready," in 1850 at the city hall in Chicago. Lincoln's memorialization of Taylor's accomplishments outlined his military service but failed to mention his own participation in the Black Hawk War. It's curious that Lincoln demurred in connecting this early military service that both he and Taylor had in common. On further reflection, it seems that the careful orator had decided it best not to include his militia service prominently in his autobiographical narrative.

SITES AND MUSEUMS NEAR SPRINGFIELD, ILLINOIS

ABRAHAM LINCOLN PRESIDENTIAL LIBRARY AND MUSEUM
A model for presidential libraries and detailed museum design, the Lincoln Presidential Library and Museum may be one of the most important historic attractions outside Washington, D.C. The exhibits provide an immersive, experiential journey through Lincoln's life and death.

Museum
212 North Sixth Street
Springfield, IL, 62701
(217) 558-8844

Library
112 North Sixth Street
Springfield, IL, 62701
(217) 558-8844

———

LINCOLN'S NEW SALEM STATE HISTORIC SITE
The State of Illinois has re-created the frontier of New Salem to approximate the village as it may have appeared in the 1830s. Open from May to October, the well-designed museum provides displays of Lincoln's early life and his trials in exploring various careers, from storekeeper to surveyor, lawyer and politician. The serene woodlands and timid waters of the Sangamon River are a half-hour drive from Springfield, Illinois.

15588 History Lane
Petersburg, IL, 62675
(217) 632-4000
lincolnsnewsalem.com

Lincoln's New Salem State Historic Site. Re-creation of Lincoln's home of Sangamon, outside Petersburg, Illinois.

YOUNG LINCOLN MURAL
Artist Michael J. Mayosky builds on his mural of Black Hawk in Fort Atkinson, Wisconsin, with this pixilated mural of a young Abe Lincoln.

109 North Fifth Street
Springfield, IL, 62701

The Captain, a bronze statue of Abraham Lincoln created by Leonard Crunelle and dedicated in 1930. Lincoln gazes southward across the Rock River. A few paces away is a re-creation of Dixon's cabin. Dixon, Illinois.

Left: Battle Ground Memorial Park, near Stillman's Run battle site. Dedicated in 1901. Stillman Valley, Illinois.

Below: Black Hawk War Monument, Black Hawk Battlefield Park, Kent, Illinois. The monument was dedicated in 1887 to American combatants killed during two engagements in the Kellogg's Grove area.

Opposite: Tombstones of militia members from the Battle of Kellogg's Grove. Black Hawk War Monument, Black Hawk Battlefield Park.

LINCOLN'S TIMELINE IN THE BLACK HAWK WAR, 1832

March 9	*Sangamon Journal* publishes Lincoln's letter of candidacy to be Illinois state representative, New Salem, Illinois.
April 7	Lincoln volunteers for the Illinois Militia and is elected captain of his unit at Dallas Scott Farm.
April 22–28	Lincoln resides at Beardstown and drills with the militia.
April 29	Illinois Militia departs for the Yellow Banks.
May 5	Camp is established at Yellow Banks.
May 7	Militia joins large mustering of forces near Rock Island and Saukenuk.
May 10	March to Prophetstown along Rock River.
May 11	American forces find Prophetstown abandoned. The village is burned, and the soldiers march to Dixon's Ferry.
May 24	Camp is made near Capa's Village, near today's Sycamore, Illinois.
May 25	March to the outskirts of Paw Paw Grove.

May 27	Arrive in Ottawa, Illinois. Lincoln's company is relieved of service. Lincoln renews service for a twenty-day extension under Captain Elijah Ilse.
June 7	Company arrives back at Dixon's Ferry.
June 8	March to Galena and arrive at Apple River Fort the evening of the ninth.
June 11	Depart Apple River Fort for Dixon's Ferry.
June 13	Arrive at Dixon's Ferry.
June 16	At Fort Wilbourn, Lincoln reenlists for another thirty days of service with Captain Jacob Early.
June 22	Arrive at Dixon's Ferry.
June 25	Depart for Kellogg's Grove and arrives at the site of the aftermath of recent skirmishes.
June 28	Return to Dixon's Ferry.
June 29	Aftermath of Stillman's Run. Company searches for American casualties on the battlefield.
July 1	Camp at Turtle Village, near present-day Beloit, Wisconsin.
July 2	Camp at the confluence of Yahara and Rock River, near Indianford, Wisconsin.
July 3	Scouting south of Lake Koshconong.
July 6	Travel along Rock River to Whitewater River, near Fort Atkinson.
July 8	Camp on Whitewater River at Burnt Village.
July 10	Near the mouth of Whitewater River, Lincoln's company is mustered out.
July 15	At Peoria, Illinois, Lincoln and Harrison break away from the other members of Early's company. They purchase a canoe and continue home.
July 17	Near Havana, George Harrison and Lincoln sell their canoe and continue home on foot.
August 4	Lincoln delivers campaign speech at courthouse in Springfield, Illinois.
August 6	Lincoln loses the election.

THE TREMBLING LANDS TO THE FOUR LAKES

From Fort Atkinson to Madison

*Black Hawk held: In reason
land cannot be sold,
only things to be carried away,
and I am old.*

*Young Lincoln's general moved,
pawpaw in bloom,
and to this day, Black Hawk,
reason has small room.*

*—Lorine Niedecker, Fort Atkinson native and poet, 1903–1970 (reprinted
with permission given by Bob Arnold, literary executor for the estate of Lorine
Niedecker)*

*Be assured every possible exertion will be made to destroy the Enemy crippled as
they must be with their wounded and families as well as their want of provision
supplies.*
*—July 24 letter to General Henry Atkinson from Colonel Henry Dodge,
Command, Mounted Volunteers*

The Battle of Stillman's Run was a pyrrhic victory for Black Hawk's British Band. The battle caused each side to pause and reconsider what the next course of action would be. After learning that his hopes of receiving aid from the British and other Native American tribes would not materialize, Black Hawk resigned himself to giving up his cause and leading his followers back across the Mississippi to Iowa. Instead, due to the accidental Battle of Stillman's Run, Black Hawk found himself turned from a supplicant to American power to victor in a complete rout of the Illinois volunteers. General Atkinson—or the "White Beaver," as he was known by the Native Americans—found himself likewise stymied by a situation that had degraded from a nuisance to a full-blown war. His inability to control the unruly Illinois Militia forces had led to an embarrassing military rout.

After the battle on Stillman's Run on May 14, Black Hawk traveled east, on the south side of the Rock River, toward present-day Beloit, Wisconsin. Following the Battle of Stillman's Run and his people's flight into present-day Wisconsin, Black Hawk noted in his autobiography, "I did not know where to go to find a place of safety for my women and children, but expected to find a good harbor about the head of Rock river. I concluded to go there, and thought my best route would be to go round the head of Kishwacokee, so that the Americans would have some difficulty if they attempted to follow us."

For the next two months, Black Hawk's followers would remain hidden somewhere east of the Four Lakes area (today's Madison, Wisconsin) and the Trembling Lands from Fort Atkinson to the northern reaches of the tributaries of the Rock River. While the elders, women and children attempted to subsist in a harsh environment, Black Hawk vacillated about his next course of action. He would lead raids into the more heavily populated Lead Region near Galena, Illinois, and Mineral Point, Wisconsin, while trying to rally other tribes to his cause. It would be more than two months until the full forces met again at the Battle of Wisconsin Heights on July 21, 1832.

While no major skirmishes took place in the area, outside of one casualty and a few incidents of friendly fire on the American side, the area was notably marked by the conflict. In 1832, both sides struggled to survive in the terrain while strategizing on their next move. The area was the gateway to the Trembling Lands, an inhospitable terrain with a sponge-like soil. It was a morass of undergrowth, marshes and paths not suitable for horses or carts.

In his autobiography, Black Hawk narrated the severity of suffering his people during this time:

Situated in a swampy, marshy country (which had been selected in consequence of the great difficulty required to gain access thereto), there was but little game of any sort to be found, and fish were equally scarce. The great distance to any settlement, and the impossibility of bringing supplies therefrom, if any could have been obtained, deterred our young men from making further attempts. We were forced to dig roots and bark trees, to obtain something to satisfy hunger and keep us alive. Several of our old people became so reduced, as to actually die with hunger! Learning that the army had commenced moving and fearing that they might come upon and surround our encampment, I concluded to remove our women and children across the Mississippi, that they might return to the Sac nation again. Accordingly, on the next day we commenced moving, with five Winnebagoes acting as our guides, intending to descend the Wisconsin.

Atkinson's delay in confronting Black Hawk caused harm to his reputation and ultimately his command. Conflicting reports from friendly tribal sources, scouts and spies gave Atkinson little accurate information on which to act.

On July 3, 1832, while ensconced in the muck and brambles of the Bark River outside the future settlement of Fort Atkinson, the command of the campaign against the British Band was transferred to Brevet Major General Winfield Scott. At the time, Scott was already a seasoned military campaigner.

However, Scott was in Buffalo, New York, hundreds of miles from the conflict. As Scott mustered his forces, he directed his officers to "take care that the rules of war, or selected articles, be read on the passage to Chicago" and that "he positively prohibits, under the highest penalties of law, as he does, all mutilating and scalping of prisoners." The general's early orders after being placed in charge of the campaign show a single-mindedness in bringing a needed order and militarily bearing to the field. He warned his officers to remember that "a few inconsiderate or worthless individuals might, if not warned and checked, bring odium on the whole army, those barbarian practices are denounced in advance."

Relieved of his command but still in charge of the field operations until Scott's arrival, General Atkinson had to feed, protect and maintain order with his own troops and irregular Illinois Militia volunteers. Atkinson's written response to General Scott a few days later on July 9, 1832, shows a sense of relief that he had "been advised by the Secretary of War, of your [Scott's] approach with a large body of troops to put an end to this perplexing and difficult Indian War." Atkinson demonstrated a very maudlin first correspondence to the person who would soon be his replacement. However, he couldn't help but warn General Scott of the dire conditions of the field: "The country is so cut up with prairie, wood and swamp, that it is extremely difficult to approach them. Indeed, many parts of the country for miles is entirely unpassable, even on foot."

Atkinson's efforts to make sense of the terrain around the Bark, White and Rock Rivers continued to elude him. He wrote to the secretary of war on July 10 that he had again tried to commence in pursuit of the British Band, but "after being baffled on his trail through swamps for the last three days, I have been compelled to suspend my operations for the want of supplies." With the demotion of standing and the prospect of Regular Army troops on their way to finalize the Black Hawk War, Atkinson began to relieve his haggard, weary and hungry volunteers.

As the decommissioned Illinois Militia members returned to their homes, General Atkinson prepared his remaining forces and busied himself in stabilizing supply lines and preparing for the relief that new troops and a new commander promised. Little did he know that the polished troops from the east would not arrive. Their transit from Buffalo, New York, across the Great Lakes would turn into an ordeal more harrowing than any that Atkinson's troops would face. More of Scott's soldiers would end up perishing trying to reach Chicago than the number that died during the actual fighting of the Black Hawk War. General Scott would end up playing no role in the conflict. The Black Hawk War would not be settled by a decorous, freshly trained army led by the charismatic General Scott. Atkinson would be forced to soldier on and confront Black Hawk himself.

SITES AND MUSEUMS NEAR THE ILLINOIS AND WISCONSIN STATE LINE

LOGAN MUSEUM OF ANTHROPOLOGY
Situated between a series of conical mounds, Beloit College's Logan Museum of Anthropology offers self-guided tours and student-led programs throughout the year. On display are faculty-collected materials from First Nations and thorough archaeological research.

700 College Street
Beloit, WI, 53511
beloit.edu/museum/logan

———

LINCOLN TALLMAN HOUSE
The public is welcome to tour the home (built in 1857) that Lincoln visited. Tours provide information on the daily life and leisure of settlers to the Rock River Valley.

440 North Jackson Street
Janesville, WI, 53548
(608) 756-4509
rchs.us

———

BLACK HAWK MURAL AND LINCOLN PLAQUE, DOWNTOWN JANESVILLE
Janesville honored Black Hawk's connection and the Native American heritage of the area by contracting with noted muralist Jeff Henriquez. Next to the mural is a plaque marking the site of the former auditorium where Lincoln spoke in 1858.

29 South Main Street
Janesville, WI, 53545

Jeff Henriquez's mural of Black Hawk, created in 2019. Downtown Janesville, Wisconsin.

———

Illinois Militia members, including Abraham Lincoln, camped in this general area. Storrs Lake, Milton, Wisconsin.

MILTON HOUSE MUSEUM
Built at the crossroads of two major American Indian footpaths, the Milton House was established by Joseph Goodrich, who came to the area in 1839. Goodrich's community became a center of abolitionism. He built a three-story hotel and stagecoach stop on the property in 1845. The Milton House is Wisconsin's only documented stop on the Underground Railroad and a registered National Historic Landmark. The museum today includes frontier and local history, as well as tours of the underground passage to the pioneer cabin that played a role in assisting fugitive slaves.

18 South Janesville Street
Milton, WI, 53563
miltonhouse.org

At the intersection of two major paths established by American Indians. The octagonal Milton House was founded at the site in 1844. Museum, Milton, Wisconsin. *Photo by Leo Strand.*

STORRS LAKE, MILTON, WISCONSIN

Lincoln camped here. Granted, it was with one thousand troops, and the exact location isn't known for sure. But a veritable city formed on the banks of Storrs Lake in early July during one of the largest massing of troops.

The lake is a busy fishing hub with pier access and paved parking lot. The more than 750-acre Storrs Lake Wildlife Area provides a few easy loop trails that allow visitors to explore the area. The forest cover of shagbark hickory and burr oaks provides a reprieve from the nearby highways and industry. The park is bisected by the Ice Age Trail and serves as a convenient home base for day hikers.

FORT ATKINSON, WISCONSIN

Fort Atkinson was named after General Atkinson's hastily constructed fortifications in 1832 and embraces its role during the Black Hawk War.

A citizen of Fort Atkinson would be hard-pressed to go a day without being reminded of the Black Hawk War. The symbol of Black Hawk is represented through the iconography of the city. Infants born at the local hospital would likely be attended to by a nurse who graduated from Blackhawk Technical College.

Each spring, youth and families take part in the Rendezvous, a reenactment of the early fur trading days. The festival takes place in a stockade that was built to resemble the original fort. Reclaimed telephone poles embedded in the ground make up the outer walls, interior blockades and a few buildings, including a rough general store and jail. While not placed in the exact location of Atkinson's original stockade, you can't help but feel a bit of excitement as you squeeze between the beaten submerged poles and into the center of the fort.

The fort motif is present throughout the city. The welcoming signs off the highway are clad in miniature hewn-log stockades. The city's official logo has adopted the Lincoln Log look, as have a number of businesses, including a popular restaurant. The high school students learn how to "Teach Me How to Blackhawk" as they cheer on their sports team and display their

Welcome sign at the entrance to Fort Atkinson, Wisconsin. *Photo by Leo Strand.*

community pride in being Blackhawks. The dance is a take on collegiate versions of videos often played at freshman orientations. The "Teach Me How to Blackhawk" endeavor, launched by an enterprising student as a fundraiser, has amassed more than eleven thousand hits on YouTube.

During the summer, as a resident of Fort Atkinson, you would head out to Black Hawk Island and launch your pontoon boat into Lake Koshkonong for some fishing and pleasure boating. The lake, or really a broad widening of the Rock River, was a traditional gathering ground for Winnebagos and Potawatomis. The shallows have provided sustenance to tribes, and the banks held seasonal harvest settlements as late as the 1930s.

Adults in Fort Atkinson can enjoy a local beer, including Tyranena Brewery's Black Hawk Porter, which is brewed just down the road in Lake Mills. Citizens traversing the main thoroughfare over the Rock River will be able to admire two striking bronze statues of an American Indian figure, leaning over the side of the Milwaukee Street Bridge as if giving an offering to the river or lighting the way for those below. These sculptures, the *Kneeling Indian*, were created by local artist Gerald P. Sawyer. Eventually, as a resident of Fort Atkinson, you may want to check into the retirement community, Black Hawk Senior Residence. Observant tourists to downtown will notice the hidden Black Hawk mural by Michael Mayosky, peeking off the third-floor of Blackhawk Senior Residence on 1 Milwaukee Avenue.

Black Hawk mural by Michael Mayosky on the side of the Black Hawk Senior Residence. Downtown, Fort Atkinson, Wisconsin.

HOARD HISTORICAL MUSEUM
Named after the noted dairy entrepreneur and publisher, the Hoard Museum is the home to permanent exhibits on the Black Hawk War and Abraham Lincoln's role in the conflict. The Abraham Lincoln library and exhibit room include numerous items from the era. The museum maintains a permanent exhibit on effigy mounds and the Mississippian Culture. The Lincoln area includes information and materials from the Black Hawk War. The active volunteer organization hosts numerous annual programs and welcomes inquiries from guests planning visits to the area. The museum is free.

401 Whitewater Avenue
Fort Atkinson, WI, 53538
hoardmuseum.org

LINCOLN HILL, COLD SPRING, WISCONSIN
A plaque notes the traditional site of Lincoln's honorary discharge from the militia. The noted ethnologist and photographer Edward Curtis would be born in Cold Spring decades after the Black Hawk War. Curtis did

Lincoln Hill. General area of where Abraham Lincoln was honorably discharged from the Illinois Militia. Cold Spring, Wisconsin.

not linger long in Wisconsin, as his family moved to Minnesota early in his childhood. Curtis would devote his life to capturing images and cultural history of American Indians throughout North America. He was very interested in capturing traditions and people who had no or very little contact with Europeans and Americans. Curtis noted that his works attempted to "give a more intimate view of Indian life in the old days… and call attention to the great divergencies of Indian life, and the striking differences in dress and habits."

Cold Spring Creamery Park
N1501 County Road N
Cold Spring, WI, 53190

————

JEFFERSON TAMARACK SWAMP WILDLIFE AREA
Sedge and moss thickets in this sprawling wildlife area may provide the best example of the inhospitable landscape that the British Band utilized to thwart General Atkinson. Visitors should arrive prepared, and be warned that poison ivy and poison sumac are present. There are three public access parking spots along County Road Y.

4265 County Road Y
Jefferson, WI, 53549

Jefferson Tamarack Swamp State Natural Area sign. Remnant of terrain that was dubbed the "Trembling Lands" during the Black Hawk War. Jefferson County, Wisconsin.

BURNT VILLAGE PARK
An abandoned Winnebago village was the site of one of the largest musters of American forces during the conflict. The small rest area provides access to the boggy and flood-prone creek. The nearby Bark River Road is a scenic route to reach the attractions in Fort Atkinson.

N2028 County Highway N
Fort Atkinson, WI, 53538

LAKE MILLS, WISCONSIN
It is commonly thought that the Black Hawk Band crossed through the Lake Mills area. However, much of the band's movements north of the Rock River remain elusive. It's very well possible that at least a portion of the group was in the area or passed nearby. A plaque noting the Black Hawk War is on display in the city square.

LAKE GENEVA, FONTANA AND WILLIAMS BAY, WISCONSIN
In her autobiographical book, *Wau-Bun*, Juliette Kinzie (1806–1870) described her arrival at Geneva Lake and the large village of Potawatomis near present-day Fontana:

> *We descended a long, sloping knoll, and by a sudden turn came full in view of the beautiful sheet of water. Bold, swelling hills jutted forward into the blue expanse, or retreated slightly to afford a green, level nook, as a resting-place for the foot of man. On the nearer shore stretched a bright, gravelly beach, through which course here and there a pure, sparkling rivulet to join the larger sheet of water. On a rising ground, at the foot of one of the bold bluffs in the middle distance, a collection of neat wigwams formed, with their surrounding gardens, no unpleasant feature in the picture.*

Chief Big Foot and the Potawatomis did not openly commit to assisting the British Band during the war of 1832; however, American forces were suspicious of potential misinformation and covert support of the British

Band. The Potawatomis were compelled to submit to a burdensome treaty in 1833 in Chicago that would effectively remove their communities from the region. Members would be pressured to leave their lands in Wisconsin for territory in Kansas and, eventually, Oklahoma.

Glimpses of the environment that Kinzie described in *Wau-Bun* can be experienced at the nearby Big Foot State Park, which is named after the Potawatomi chief. The lakeshore path around Geneva Lake also holds a unique vantage from which to experience the beauty of Geneva Lake.

GENEVA LAKE PEDESTRIAN PATH

The Geneva Lake path allows public access to the shoreline, and property owners must maintain access for pedestrians. However, there are only a handful of public lands from which you can enter or exit the path. So ambulators should plan accordingly, bring snacks and water and be warned that bathroom facilities are few and far between. The entire length of the path is more than twenty-six miles. Parts are unpaved and steep. Each property owner approaches his or her stewardship of the path differently. Sections vary from bare earth to cobblestone or paved sidewalk. During the summer months, the sections from Big Foot State Park to the Lake Geneva Library and from the library to Williams Bay are the most popular and accessible. Travelers will find an occasional bench, periodic artwork and glimpses of the lifestyles of the rich and famous.

BIG FOOT STATE PARK

Visitors are required to pay a daily fee or have an annual Wisconsin State Park sticker while on the shoreline of Geneva Lake with respect to hiking and campsites.

1550 South Lake Shore Drive
Lake Geneva, WI, 53147
dnr.wi.gov/topic/parks/name/bigfoot

Geneva Lake Museum
This history museum in downtown Lake Geneva includes displays of Potawatomi artifacts from the area, with a larger focus on the city's history since American settlement.

255 Mill Street
Lake Geneva, WI, 53147
(262) 248-6060
genevalakemuseum.org

LEAD REGION RAIDS

Meanwhile Chief Shabbona was riding far
To warn the homes which lay toward the east,
Guiding his course by some familiar star,
And sparing not himself nor faithful beast,
However much the labor of his task increased.
—*Jas R.E. Craighead and his telling of the Black Hawk War*
in Spenserian verse, 1930

You say, go to war and take your revenge [on the Sauk and Fox]. *We came to*
do so, and you sent us with a little man [Colonel William Hamilton]. *We*
followed him a great way over large wagon roads that were very hard, and our
moccasins are worn out and our feet sore; we can walk no further. We had starved
until we were tired—we did not want to go any further.
—*meeting with General Street and Sioux chief Larc, June 22, 1832, at Prairie*
du Chien, Galenian, July 11, 1832

With General Atkinson's forces bogged down in the marshes and wetlands along the Rock, Whitewater and Bark Rivers, Black Hawk set out with a cohort of warriors to harass the communities in the Lead Region. In his autobiography, Black Hawk spurred his followers on with these words:

Braves and warriors: These are the medicine bags of our forefather, Muk-
a-tá-quet, who was the father of the Sac nation. They were handed down

to the great war chief of our nation, Na-ná-ma-kee, who has been at war with all the nations of the lakes and all the nations of the plains, and have never yet been disgraced! I expect you all to protect them! After the ceremony was over and our feasting done, I started with about two hundred warriors…and we started for Mos-co-ho-co-y-nak [Apple River].

As Cecil Eby noted in his book *That Disgraceful Affair the Black Hawk War*, Stillman's Run and the rout of the militia ignited a series of violent confrontations across the state of Illinois and the Northwest Territory. Disagreements and grudges between American Indian communities and the new settlers erupted into coldblooded violence. Many of these acts didn't involve members of the "British Band," but they certainly further eroded any sense of safety that the pioneers may have held. These ancillary conflicts included the salacious murder of a group of pioneers and the imprisonment of Rachel and Sylvia Hall. A group of Potawatomis and Sauks murdered fifteen settlers and took the two teenage girls hostage. The two survivors would later be held for a time at the British Band's camp. Black Hawk credited the presence of the two Sauks in preserving the lives of the Hall girls. Rachel and Sylvia would be released to the Americans at Fort Blue Mounds, thanks to the negotiations of Ho-Chunk chief White Crow.

The "Indian Creek Massacre" was the culmination of a long-standing conflict between pioneers and tribal members. Rachel and Sylvia Hall shared after the incident that they were familiar with the Potawatomi members involved in the attack. Fifteen settlers were murdered in the incident, and the harrowing tale was quickly written up into a book.

The impact of these raids sent a wave of terror throughout the frontier. It spurred miners to abandon their claims and seek shelter in hastily constructed forts. The editor of the *Galenian* noted that he was enlisting in the militia in order to "tell you a good story about our war and give you a lecture on Indian killing," as well as "exchange my sword and short gun for a goose quill."

Black Hawk orchestrated a series of raids into the Lead Region to distract the main body of General Atkinson's forces. In Galena, the miners had abandoned their claims and were holed up in defensive forts. Horatio Newhall shared with his brother the terror experienced by the populace. Horatio noted a false alarm sounded late at night by the firing of the alarm gun, which caused a great frenzy. In a panic, "seven hundred women and children…some with dresses on, and some with none; some with shoes, some barefoot," rushed from their homes to the fort. The "women and children

Indian Campaign of 1832: Map of the Country, by Colonel Edwin Rose, 1832. *Courtesy of the Map Library at the University of Illinois at Urbana–Champaign.*

were screaming from one end of the town to the other." The preparations were well earned, as on June 24 the Apple River Fort was attacked by Black Hawk and his warriors. The *Galenian* recounted the battle:

Appleriver Fort was attacked last night by 150 Indians. They continued the fire for about 3 quarters of an hour. F. Dixon and Mr. Welch started to go as an express to Gen. Atkinson, and after passing Apple river fort about 14 miles from this place, were fired on by a party of Indians, when Welch fell from his horse badly, though not mortally, wounded. The Indians were very numerous in all directions, Mr. Dixon assisted Welch to mount his horse again, and they retreated amidst the fire of the Indians to the fort.... Mr. Kirkpatrick, who was at the fort during the fight, says that every man, woman and child took an active part in the defense of the fort. They killed one man in the fort, by the name of G.W. Herclerode, who was shot in the head while climbing above the picket to get a fair shot at an Indian.

With the inhabitants terrorized inside the fort, Black Hawk reasoned in his autobiography that "finding that these people could not all be killed, without setting fire to their houses and fort, I thought it prudent to be content with what flour, provisions, cattle and horses we could find, than to set fire to their buildings as the light would be seen at a distance and the army might suppose that we were in the neighborhood."

Governor Dodge's prominence as a leader in the conflict was forged by his actions at the Battle of the Pecatonica River, also referred to as the Battle of Horse Shoe Bend. Following the British Band's attacks on the Apple River Fort, Dodge set out with a small force to quell the panic-stricken settlements. The Battle of the Pecatonica River took place a few miles from the settlement of William Hamilton (son of Alexander Hamilton), or present-day Wiota, Wisconsin, and south of Dodgeville. Dodge's status with the populace and General Atkinson was greatly elevated following his mustering of forces and leadership in the first militia victory of the conflict. At the windy creek bog, Dodge accomplished a total victory of killing nine Kickapoo warriors, with three of Dodge's men suffering mortal wounds, according to the June 18, 1832 *Galenian*:

Mr. Editor—You have often spoken in the highest terms of General Dodge, and expressed a wish that he might be placed in command of the army, which is to decide the fate of this country in concluding the present war. I have, as often, wondered that you would thus speak of a man untried, and, as yet, somewhat inexperienced in Indian warfare; but the victory which has just been achieved and the manner in which the battle was conducted by General Dodge, have inspired me, and I believe convinced the whole community, that your confidence was not misplaced. With such a Commander as General Dodge and such men as have proved their valor in the late charge, I would not fear to go and face the enemy, though twice our numbers. Nothing so much conduces to infuse courage into men, as the full confidence in their commander. Victory has once been achieved, and from this time hence, let our motto be, VICTORY OR DEATH; and our watch word FINAL EXTERMINATION.

SITES AND MEMORIALS OF BLACK HAWK WAR RAIDS

BLACK HAWK MEMORIAL PARK
Managed by Lafayette County, the battle site of the Pecatonica River, or Horse Shoe Bend, is a community park and campground. Visitors can walk

or drive through the terrain of the battle. A local community group hosts the Bloody Lake Rendezvous almost annually.

2995 County Trunk Y
Woodford, WI, 53599
(608) 465-3390

———

APPLE RIVER FORT STATE HISTORIC SITE
The town of Elizabeth is named in honor of three women, all named Elizabeth, who valiantly rallied the community during the Apple River Fort attack. The reconstructed fort provides educational and historic programs. A museum and visitors' center welcomes guests a block before the roadway to the fort.

311 East Myrtle
Elizabeth, IL, 61028
appleriverfort.org

Apple River Fort State Historic Site's welcome center. Elizabeth, Illinois.

Reconstruction of Apple River Fort. Elizabeth, Illinois.

Battle of the Pecatonica, or Horse Shoe Bend. Black Hawk Memorial Park. Woodford, Wisconsin.

KELLOGG'S GROVE
High among rolling farmland, Kellogg's Grove was built along the Native American trail that ran from Peoria to Prairie du Chien. The original structures from 1832 are no longer standing. The individual graves of the American militia and soldiers who were killed during the two battles near Kellogg's Grove and Yellow Creek on June 15 and June 25 were disinterred and reburied at this memorial. In 1887, the monument was consecrated. The pillar of native limestone has a base of carved stone cannonballs. The names of the Americans who fell in the area are inscribed on individual graves around the memorial.

14109 West Black Hawk Road
Kent, IL, 61044

LOWDEN STATE PARK
The Eternal Indian statue. Lorado Taft's colossal fifty-foot statue was unveiled in 1911.

1411 North River Road
Oregon IL, 61061
(815) 732-6828

CHICAGO AND CHOLERA

Winfield Scott Takes Command

The Citizens of Saint Louis on the night of Friday, the 3ʳᵈ of August, to take into consideration a day of Fasting, Humiliation and Prayer, and to implore Divine Providence to avert from our city the threatened calamity of Asiatic Cholera. Resolved, That we recommend to all the churches and congregations in our city, an entire day of suspension of worldly business. Proposed by Reverend Mr. Porrs and Chair, Edward Bates, Esquire.
—Missouri Republican, St. Louis, August 7, 1832

I only want to get one trophy first—not withstanding General Scott has positively prohibited scalping, etc, yet if I bring a Red Rascal I think I'll manage to have his head off before he dies, which will not be mutilating him you know and I'll have to cut off his head to kill him and having his noodle I can take his scalp with impunity. Give my love to all, Your affect Son Lewis.
—Lewis Clark, in a letter to his father, Superintendent of Indian Affairs William Clark

Thirty years after the end of the Black Hawk War, President Abraham Lincoln would draw on General Winfield Scott's military experience and strategy as he grappled with the great American Civil War. A graduate of West Point, Winfield Scott was a consummate by-the-book commander who strove to bring order, professionalism and precision to military affairs.

Before Scott would gain the moniker "Old Fuss and Feathers," he was assigned as the commander of the American armies during the Black Hawk War. Scott would spend decades after the Black Hawk War leveling U.S.

forces into conflicts with Native American communities. Due to General Atkinson's dithering and delay in pursuing the British Band, President Andrew Jackson ordered Winfield Scott to depart from the eastern Great Lakes with a professionally trained force of American soldiers to bring Black Hawk into abeyance.

General Scott quickly readied his command. Even as the threat of a potential outbreak of disease, Asiatic cholera, was beginning to appear on the East Coast, he was not deterred. Cholera did not discriminate— it afflicted both Americans and First Nation peoples. In 1832, the disease could not be averted through immunization. The waterborne bacteria was transmitted through poor sanitation and contaminated water supplies. General Winfield Scott believed that his training of preventing and treating cholera was sufficient to ward off any danger of the outbreak.

The symptoms and severe consequences of the affliction are described in the book *Cholera: Facts and Conclusions as to Its Nature in 1866* by Henry Hartshorne (1823–1897):

> *An acute systemic epidemic disorder, not contagious, but produced under certain local circumstances by an unknown specific cause. Symptoms being, a premonitory, painless, and mostly watery diarrhea of variable duration, followed by vomiting, watery and increased diarrhea, with weakness, coldness, intense thirst, difficult of breathing, loss of voice, cold breath, cramps, disappearance of pulse, and a blue or livid and shrunken aspect of the skin; which symptoms may end in death in from ten minutes to forty-eight hours. Or, in a partial reaction, low fever the result of which is either death in a few days or recovery in a week or two.*

Confident in his rudimentary instruction in medicine from Surgeon Mower, who had shared with Scott his theories on the treatment of the disease, General Scott departed New York State with 950 troops on board four cramped ships. This force, trained in the profession and discipline of the art of war, was hoped to be the tipping point in bringing an ordered resolution to the conflict with Black Hawk and his followers.

In Scott's autobiography, written with assistance and in the third person in 1864, the author glosses over the horrendous suffering his command suffered during the journey. Scott's troops began to show signs of being infected with cholera within a few days of embarking. The onslaught struck the only surgeon in the company, who, Scott noted, coped by drinking too much wine and soon succumbed to the sickness.

Scott was not deterred. He continued the journey, keeping his charges in order through sheer will and even at one point ordering soldiers not to get sick. Scott's determination was no match for the pestilence of bacterial infection.

As his fleet sailed on, cholera continued to infect the troops. Confined to close quarters and with poor sanitation, the disease quickly took hold. General Scott was forced to continually drop the stricken onto the shore. Soldiers were left with thin instructions and thinner resources for their recuperation. Of the 950 who departed New York State, only 350 arrived in Chicago. In General Zachary Taylor's autobiography, he estimated Scott's force as high as 1,500 who left Old Fort Comfort by ship, with 200 deaths attributed to cholera.

John Wenworth's reminiscences of serving on the *Henry Clay* was printed in 1881 by the Chicago Historical Society: "The disease became so violent and alarming on board the Henry Clay that nothing like discipline could be observed; everything in the way of subordination ceased. As soon as the steamer came to the dock each man sprang on shore, hoping to escape from a scene so terrifying and appalling. Some fled to the fields, some to the woods, while other lay down in the streets and under the cover of the river bank, where most of them died unwept and alone."

The *Niles' Weekly Register* newspaper on July 28, 1832, reported a remarkably horrific scene: "The desserters, scattered all over the country, some have died in the woods and their bodies have been devoured by wolves. The straggling survivors are occasionally seen marching, some of them know now whither, with their knapsacks on their backs, shunned by the terrified inhabitants, as the source of a mortal pestilence."

The speed of Scott's marathon journey—an 1,800-mile water voyage across the Great Lakes in eighteen days—was laudable. However, the fact that his fighting capacity was decimated calls into question Scott's effectiveness. After the remaining troops arrived in Chicago, the city's inhabitants literally abandoned their homes.

In the August 11, 1832 *Niles' Weekly Register*, an officer serving on the *Sheldon Thompson* described the horror of the voyage across the Great Lakes as cholera swept through the troops:

> *Men died in six hours after being in perfect health. The steerage was crowded with the dying, and new cases were appearing on the deck, when the demon entered the cabin....Sergeant Heyl was well at 9 o'clock in the morning—he was at the bottom of Lake Michigan by 7 o'clock in the*

afternoon. I had to remove all the sick men to the shore; I had scarcely got through my task, when I was thrown down on the deck almost as suddenly as if shot. I felt a sudden rush of blood from my feet upwards, and as it rose, my veins grew cold and my blood curdled. I was seized with nausea at the stomach and a desire to vomit. My legs and hands were cramped with violent pain. The doctor gave me 8 grains of opium and make me rub my legs as fast as I could; he also made me drink a tumbler and a half full of raw brandy, and told me if I did not throw up the opium I would certainly be relieved.

General Winfield Scott would leave his remaining forces in Chicago to recuperate, while he and a handful of guides made their way north. The hoped-for discipline and order of Scott's command would not play a role in the Black Hawk War. The fight would instead be led by the frontiersman Henry Dodge and General Atkinson.

CHICAGO-AREA SITES AND MUSEUMS

FORT DEARBORN

Represented as one of the four red stars on the city of Chicago's flag, Fort Dearborn played a role in the Black Hawk War as the landing spot for Winfield Scott's forces. No physical trace of Fort Dearborn remains, as the last portions of the original fort were incinerated during the Great Chicago Fire. The building is memorialized in the pavement on the corner of Michigan Avenue and Upper Wacker Drive. Pedestrians can walk along the outline of the former fort that has been marked across the road and sidewalks.

Michigan Avenue and Upper Wacker Drive
Chicago, Illinois

AMERICAN INDIAN CENTER INC.

Since 1953, the AIC has been a home for First Nation peoples in the Chicagoland area. With a thriving artistic and cultural center, the AIC has a robust calendar of exhibits, events and activities that welcome the

Plaque embedded in the sidewalk to designate the walls of Fort Dearborn. Downtown Chicago, Illinois.

community. Its mission is to "be the primary cultural and community resource for over 65,000 NAs in the greater Chicago metropolitan area. Chicago is home to the third largest urban NA population with over 140 tribal nations represented."

3401 West Ainslie Street
Chicago, Illinois
aicchicago.org

———

NEWBERRY LIBRARY
The preeminent private nonprofit library of the Midwest, the Newberry contains innumerous resources and primary materials from the onset of European and American migration to the Midwest. Its map collection, early American collection and the D'Arcy McNickle Center for American Indian and Indigenous Studies collection are world renowned. The Newberry

continues to provide outreach, seminars and digitization of its collections so that the community and researchers have access to its resources through online digital collections. The Newberry Library often hosts in-depth revolving exhibits and highlights the Native American traditions represented in its collections.

60 West Walton Street
Chicago, IL, 60610
newberry.org

————

CHICAGO HISTORY MUSEUM
Dedicated to the broad expanse of Chicago's exponential growth and importance in the Midwest, the Chicago History Museum includes resources and exhibits of the original Native American peoples in the region.

1601 North Clark Street
Chicago, IL, 60614-6038
chicagohistory.org

————

TRIBUNE TOWER
The Tribune Tower is bedazzled with representative stones from 150 famous architecturally significant buildings across the world—although they do not serve as any true structural support of the skyscraper. Pedestrians can walk around the building and view fragments from the Parthenon, the Pyramid of Giza, the Alamo and the Old Trading Fort at Prairie du Chien, Wisconsin. Look on the East Illinois side of the Tribune Tower for the rectangular stone from the old fort. For centuries, Prairie du Chien was a central trading and gathering location for Native American communities. Situated at the confluence of the Wisconsin and Mississippi Rivers, Prairie du Chien would never obtain prominence as a major city. It would not be until after the Black Hawk War that Chicago would become the epicenter of Midwest commerce and culture.

435 North Michigan Avenue
Chicago, Illinois

Mitchell Museum of the American Indian
North of Chicago, the Mitchell Museum of the American Indian contextualizes items in its ten-thousand-plus-piece collection. Its mission is to promote and share a deeper understanding of Native American peoples through the collection, preservation and interpretation of its traditional and contemporary art and material culture.

3001 Central Street
Evanston, IL, 60201
(847) 475-1030
mitchellmuseum.org

BATTLE OF WISCONSIN HEIGHTS

The most brilliant exhibition of military tactics that I ever witnessed—a feat of most consummate management and bravery, in the face of an enemy of greatly superior numbers. I never read of anything that could be compared with it. Had it been performed by white men, it would have been immortalized as one of the most splendid achievements in military history.
—Jefferson Finis Davis

Kellogg's Old Place, near which had perished, by the blood of our savage foe, four of our fellow citizens, Felix St. Vrain, agent for the same tribe who shed his blood.
—Galenian, *June 6, 1832*

West of the Four Lakes area and present-day Madison, Wisconsin, the American militia discovered the trail of the British Band. Near the general region of Hustisford and Watertown, Dodge's scouts finally came across clear indications that the main host of the British Band was headed north to the Wisconsin River. The Four Lakes region has been the home of the Ho-Chunk Nation for thousands of years. They had a series of villages along Four Lakes, including a large village at the mouth of Token Creek.

The path was described by Colonel Charles Whittlesey:

> *The scattering of trails of the retreating Indians were still distinct* [in September 1832, a few weeks after the war]. *Sometimes they would*

all converge into one broad and plain track, then again radiate in different directions, continually branching and spreading over the country, dwindling to a mere trace. This resulted from their method of travel, sometimes in a body, then in classes, these again subdivided, and so on, for the double purpose of deceiving their pursuers in regard to their true route, and also of dispersion and escape in case of attack. It proved one of the greatest annoyances and hindrances of the expedition.

North of the Four Lakes, the British Band attempted to cross the Wisconsin River. Across the river, near today's Sauk Prairie, there was an old Sauk village that had been abandoned as the importance of Saukenuk increased.

Black Hawk related in his autobiography how he viewed the engagement at Wisconsin Heights as a success. His main goal was to protect the noncombatants of the British Band from the American army. "With only fifty braves, I defended and accomplished my passage over the Ouisconsin, with a loss of only six men; though opposed by a host of mounted militia." He noted that a fair number of his band parted ways from the main group, either by continuing their descent of the Wisconsin or by selecting another path altogether.

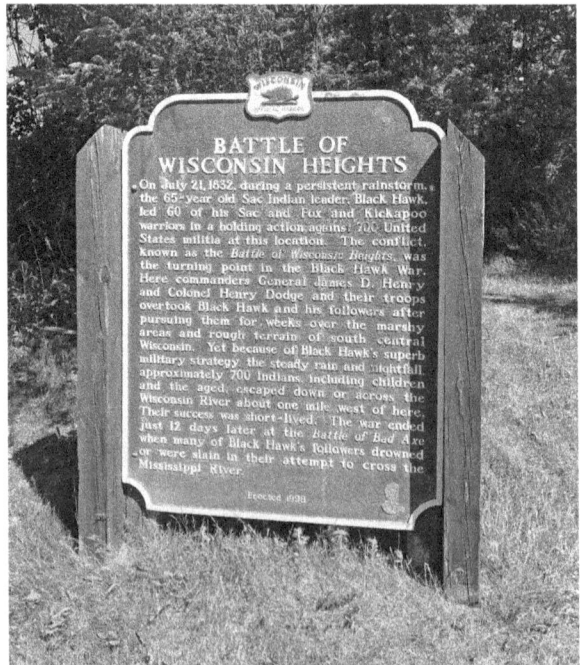

Entrance sign at the Battle of Wisconsin Heights. Sauk City, Wisconsin.

Dodge's Cabin, Dodgeville, Wisconsin. The log cabin was restored by the Dodgeville Historical Society, believed to be from Henry Dodge's settlement during the lead mining era.

Henry Dodge wrote the following description of the battle:

The Enemy raised the Yell and gulloped up within thirty yards of us, we fired on them and killed one. And wounded one or two others, when they retreated. The enemy rallied and commenced a fire on the left flank, his object was evidently to outflank us.

When the battle was over it was 7 Oclk. our men had made a force march of forty miles many of them on foot, and exposed about six hours in the rain their arms wet and out of order. Knowing that they had retreated to the river and that they had chosen their position and that we could not reach them before dark, after consulting with Genl. Henry it was agreed to defer a further attack on the enemy until the next morning. We marched from our position early in the day, and found he had crossed the river, he had left his camp in much hurry and confusion, from the appearance of the trees, bark canoes had been prepared for the purpose of crossing the Wisconsin.

Madison, Wisconsin–Area Sites and Museums

Battle at Wisconsin Heights
The Black Hawk Unit on the Lower Wisconsin State Riverway is an excellent trail and features a historic marker that describes the actual battlefield of the Battle of Wisconsin Heights. Located about three miles south of Sauk Prairie on Highway 78, the prairie restoration at the site includes notable vegetation.

dnr.wi.gov/topic/Lands/LowerWisconsin/trails.html

———

Wisconsin Historical Society Library
816 State Street
Madison, WI, 53706
wisconsinhistory.org

———

Wisconsin Historical Museum
30 North Carroll Street
Madison, WI, 53703
wisconsinhistory.org

———

University of Wisconsin–Madison
In 2019, a plaque was added near to the steps of Bascom Hill acknowledging the cultural history of First Nation communities in the region. Another, older plaque commemorates the passing of Black Hawk's band through the area. This plaque is near the Carillon on Observatory Drive, about one block behind Bascom Hall.

MASSACRE AT THE BAD AXE

From Sauk Prairie to De Soto, Wisconsin

Black Hawk and the Sacs has just reached the Mississippi. [I] was standing near Black Hawk. Black Hawk said "run and get me the white flag. I will go on board the boat." He told the men to put down their guns, and the women got behind the trees. He then hollowed [sic] to the boat, "bring me one of your canoes. I want to board your boat." He repeated this several times, and the boat fired twice.
—*Kish-kas-shoi, Sac and Fox woman, thirty-five years old, prisoner's testimony, August 19, 1832*

Black Hawk despairing of effecting an escape, hoisted the white flag, and made signs to our people to approach for a parley. Our force would not respect the flag, but commenced firing and killed 23.
—*John Kinzie , sub-agent of Indian affairs*

About four o'clock on Wednesday afternoon [August 1]…as we neared them, they raised a white flag, and endeavored to decoy us; but we were a little too old for them. After about a fifteen minute delay, giving them time to remove a few of their women and children, we let slip a six-pounder, loaded with canister, followed by a severe fire of musketry.
—*Joseph Throckmorton, captain of the ship* Warrior, *report on the Battle of the Bad Axe, August 3, 1832*

T he Battle of Wisconsin Heights would serve as the final delaying tactic before the full onslaught of American forces could confront Black Hawk's band. As the forces of Henry Dodge's militia and General Atkinson's Regular Army troops prepared to cross the Wisconsin and pursue Black Hawk, the starving and worn-out band made a frantic retreat north and west to the Mississippi River.

The terrain remained an impediment to the militia and regular forces, but it did not prove to be the untraceable morass that the Trembling Lands around the White River had been. Now that the American militia and regular forces had ascertained the location of the British Band, it was just a matter of time before a full assault would begin.

Members of the British Band began to break off from the main group. Some were too exhausted to continue and sought refuge in small groups or attempted to find shelter with friendly Winnebagos or Potawatomis in the region. More individuals attempted to flee down the Wisconsin River. General Atkinson was cognizant of this route of escape.

On July 31, General Atkinson received reports that his troops stationed along the Wisconsin River, upstream from Fort Armstrong in Prairie du Chien, had encountered individuals fleeing the aftermath of the Battle of Wisconsin Heights. Instead of crossing the river, a number had chosen to try to escape by descending the Wisconsin River. A report sent from soldiers stationed near Helena to Atkinson noted that troops had killed fifteen to twenty people attempting to flee in canoes and captured another seventeen. The report noted that the members of the British Band were "almost dying with starvation, and are mere shadows, with a few rags scarcely sufficient to hide their nakedness."

The American forces resupplied and began crossing the Wisconsin River at Helena. The homes and half-built shot tower provided the material to construct rafts to transport their supplies across the river. The path of the British Band was now clearly evident to the Americans, who followed the path of abandoned materials and elders and children too exhausted to continue.

On August 1, the British Band reached the Mississippi River near Bad Axe. Their attempts to construct canoes to escape across the river were thwarted by the passing of Joseph Throckmorton, captain of the ship *Warrior*. Black Hawk attempted to surrender to the Americans. Instead, the troops fired on the British Band, who had hoisted a white flag. After a short engagement, the *Warrior* broke off its assault to share the word of its discovery with the rest of the American troops.

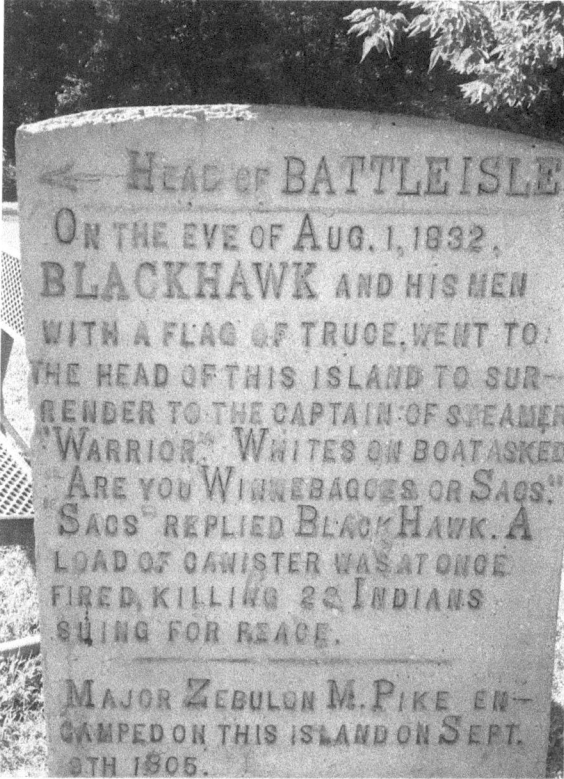

Left: Battle Isle Historic Marker, with a flag of truce. Dr. Charles V. Porter interviewed locals and documented a possible skirmish and trails of the Black Hawk War. His work in the 1880s relied on local reminiscences. Battle Isle, outside DeSoto, Wisconsin.

Below: Battle of Bad Axe Historic Marker. The Wisconsin Historical Society has added a modern interpretation of the Black Hawk War to supplement Dr. Porter's fading cement way signs. Battle Bluff, outside DeSoto, Wisconsin.

That night, Black Hawk, the Prophet and a small group left the main body of the British Band and escaped north. The next day, the remaining members were confronted by Dodge's militia members, Atkinson's regular troops and the *Warrior*. The battle, as described via personal accounts and in the August 8, 1832 reporting of the *Galenian*'s Dr. Addison Philleo, who also served as a surgeon during the battle's aftermath, has generally come to be seen as a massacre:

> *The Indians were driven by our spies from hill to hill and kept up a tolerably brisk firing from every situation commanding the ground....During this time the Brigades of Generals Alexander and Posey, were marching down the river when they fell in with another part of the enemy's army and killed and routed all that opposed them. Our whole force descended the almost perpendicular bluff and came into a low valley, heavily timbered, with a large growth of underbrush, weeds and grasses. Sloughs and deep ravines, old logs, etc., were so plentiful as to afford every facility for the enemy to make a strong defense.*
>
> *The battle lasted upwards of three hours. About 50 of the enemy's women and children were taken prisoners, and many, by accident in the battle, were killed. When the Indians were driven to the Bank of the Mississippi, some hundreds of men, women and children plunged into the river, and hoped by diving, etc, to escape the bullets of our guns; very few, however, escaped our sharpshooters. The loss on the side of the enemy never can be exactly ascertained, but according to the best computation, they must have lost in killed, upwards of 150. Our loss and killed and wounded was 27.*

The *Galenian* of August 29, 1832, reported:

> *A SCENE AT THE BATTLE OF THE BAD AXE*
> *When our troops charged the enemy in their defiles near the bank of the Mississippi, men, women and children were seen mixed together in such manner as to render it difficult to kill one, and save the other. A young [woman] of about 19 years, stood in the grass at a short distance from our line, holding her little girl in her arms, about four years old. While thus standing apparently unconcerned, a ball struck the right arm of the child above the elbow and shattering the bone, passed into the breast of its young mother which instantly felled her to the ground. She fell upon the child and confined it to the ground also. During the whole battle this babe was heard*

Battle Isle in Blackhawk Park, DeSoto, Wisconsin. Site of Black Hawk's attempt to surrender to the captain of the steamboat *Warrior*.

Battle Bluff, near DeSoto, Wisconsin. August 2019.

View of the Battle Isle and the Mississippi River from the peak of Battle Bluff. Note the near forty-five-degree slope of the hill. August 2019.

to groan and call for relief, but none had time to afford it. When however, the Indians had retreated from that spot, and the battle had nearly subsided, Lieutenant Anderson of the U.S. Army, went to the spot and took from under the dead mother her wounded daughter and brought it to the place we had selected for dressing wounds, and placed it there for surgical aid. It was soon ascertained that its arm must come off, and the operation was performed without drawing a tear or shriek. The child was eating a piece of hard biscuit during the operation. It was brought to Prairie du Chien, and we learn it has nearly recovered.

While the British Band had clearly been defeated, the American forces almost immediately became concerned about the remaining threat of First Nations in the territory. It was also unclear which tribes, clans or even families had supported the British Band.

One of the Indian agents for the Winnebagos, Joseph Street, tried to vouch for their conduct during the conflict. He outlined how the Winnebagos had remained neutral during the conflict, except for one family, who joined the British Band. Street wrote to General Atkinson, "I make this statement which is corroborated by my several letters to the Department during the war, to shew [show] you the injustice that some persons in the army seem disposed to shew towards me as well as the Indians of my agency."

However, General Atkinson was unconvinced and would a few days later chide the gathered chiefs:

The Sacs and Foxes came into your Country and while they were in your Country, you knew that they were killing the White People; still you did not drive them out. I had to march all over your Country to find them and have them driven over the Mississippi and killing half of them....I had many talks with Other Winnebagoes—they told me lies—they deceived me when they told me where to find the Sacs. You, Wah-kon Decari went to the Americans at Fort Hamilton and promised to fight with them against the Sacs—yet you came away and brought the other of your Band with you without doing anything.

Atkinson's distrust of the Winnebagos would lead to further repressive treaties and the loss of their traditional lands.

BAD AXE AND DESOTO, WISCONSIN–AREA SITES AND MUSEUMS

VERNON COUNTY HISTORICAL SOCIETY

The Vernon County Historical Society maintains a travel guide documenting the Black Hawk War sites and path. It provides free resources as well as the travel guide to aid in visiting the markers installed by Dr. Charles V. Porter, who researched the trail and battle sites in the 1880s. Porter constructed a series of cement road signs that describe the local lore of the British Band's flights through the area. The roadways start in Rising Sun, Wisconsin, and by following Highway 27 North and then Highway 82 to the West, the road roughly follows a portion of the path of the British Band.

410 South Center Avenue
P.O. Box 444
Viroqua, WI, 54665
(608) 637-7396
vernoncountyhistory.org

BLACKHAWK PARK, DESOTO, WISCONSIN

The Blackhawk Park provides free access to the main battleground of the massacre, which took place on August 2–3, 1832. It is a bit jarring to experience a battlefield site within a bustling recreational campground. Among the 150 reservable campsites, visitors can get right up to the Mississippi River and the shoreline across from Battle Isle. A historic marker next to the large group event shelter describes the massacre that transpired on the land in 1832.

U.S. Army Corps of Engineers
E590 City Road BI
DeSoto, WI, 54624
(608) 648-3314
recreation.gov

LANDMARKS, BATTLEFIELDS, MUSEUMS & FIRSTHAND ACCOUNTS

BATTLE BLUFF STATE PARK
This state-owned land does not have any amenities, trails or parking. Please review the access information with the Wisconsin Department of Natural Resources. The hike up the 480-foot-high Battle Bluff is amazingly steep and treacherous. Please be cognizant of your own skill level as well as the potential to roll a few hundred feet down a forty-five-degree incline.

———

WISCONSIN STATE NATURAL AREAS PROGRAM
Visitors will have a high chance of being the only visitor on the bluff. The peak provides a breathtaking view of Battle Isle and the Mississippi River Valley.

Battle Bluff Prairie (No. 177)
dnr.wi.gov

———

THE DRIFTLESS AREA EDUCATION AND VISITORS' CENTER, LANSING, IOWA
A new visitor and information center is about a twenty-minute drive from the Battle Bluff and Battle Isle. Check its website for programming and exhibit information.

1944 Columbus Road
Lansing, IA, 52151
(563) 538-0400
allamakeecountyconservation.org

145

BLACK HAWK'S CAPTURE
AND PRAIRIE DU CHIEN, WISCONSIN

Above Dubuque the water of the Mississippi was olive-green—rich and beautiful and semi-transparent, with the sun on it. The majestic bluffs that overlook the weather, along through this region, charm one with the grace and variety of their forms, and the soft beauty of their adornment....It is all as tranquil and reposeful as dreamland, and has nothing this-worldly about it—nothing to hang a fret or a worry upon.
—Life on the Mississippi, *Mark Twain*

It is astonishing that there are not more murders and affrays at this place [Prairie du Chien], where meets such an heterogeneous mass to trade, the use of spiritous liquors being in manner restricted; but since the American has become known, such accidents are much less frequent.
—Zebulon Pike, 1806

The Prairie du Chien is the rendezvous of a number of Indians who come there in autumn to lay in winter provisions and in the spring to settle with their creditors who receive skins in payment. They are much more punctual that the whites would be if they had no other guide than the law of nature, nor any other argument than their bow and arrow, their knife and gun.
—Giacomo Constantine Beltrami, 1823

T he Winnebago Red Cloud described his people's capture of Black Hawk. A hunting party from his tribe came across the small group of Black Hawk's remaining contingent not far from the Winnebago village near present-day Bangor, Wisconsin. After confronting Black Hawk, Red Cloud convinced him to surrender. Red Cloud's band conveyed the last of those following Black Hawk and the Prophet to the Americans at Fort Crawford in Prairie du Chien on August 27, 1832.

North of the Lead Region, Prairie du Chien had for centuries served as a traditional common gathering ground of First Nations. The location of Prairie du Chien, at the confluence of the Mississippi and Wisconsin Rivers, was ideally situated as a neutral ground for trading and conducting diplomacy.

The Americans gathered close to 130 prisoners from the remnants of the British Band. The weary individuals were brought in singularly or in small groups and were questioned by the regular troops. The members who were able to cross the Mississippi at Bad Axe were pursued by the Sioux, who had been alerted by the Americans of the presence of their mutual enemy.

The interrogation of the prisoners included the women, children and warriors. The Americans needed to determine which local tribes had assisted

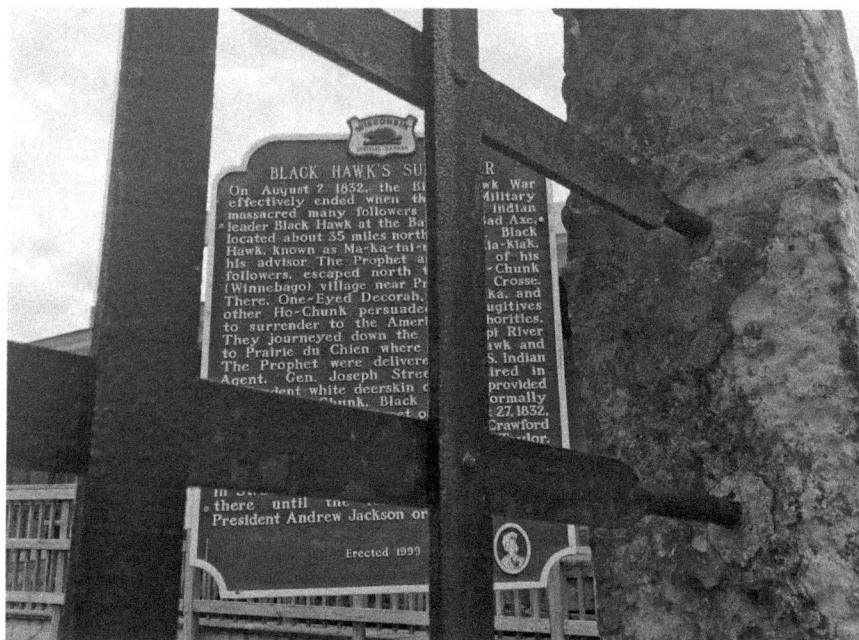

Remnant of prison bars from Fort Crawford and Black Hawk's imprisonment. Site of the second Fort Crawford, Prairie du Chien, Wisconsin.

Bronze sculpture of Black Hawk by Florence Bird at Mississippi River Sculpture Park. Prairie du Chien, Wisconsin.

the British Band, who were the key leaders of the renegade group and, if possible, to try to discover what specific individuals had been involved in the raids across the region.

In their interviews, three Sauk principals—Neopope, Ma-kauk and Ioway—noted the role that their Winnebago guide, the One-Eyed Decorah, or "the Blind," played in spurring on their fight with the Americans. Ma-kauk stated that their principal guides had been "The Prophet and the man 'the blind' with a black handkerchief over his blind eye were the principal Winnebagoes." Ioway believed that if not for the involvement of "the Blind," they would have "asked for peace above Cosh-ko-nong at White Water."

From Prairie du Chien, Jefferson Davis escorted Black Hawk via riverboat down the Mississippi River, past Galena, Rock Island and Saukenuk. The captain of the ship refused to stop at Fort Armstrong for a meeting with General Atkinson because the cholera had reached the area and he didn't want to risk infection. Black Hawk was delivered to the headquarters of the Western Army at Jefferson Barracks near St. Louis.

The *Galenian* reported within a few days of Black Hawk's capture that calm and normalcy was beginning to return to the mining region:

> *Upper Mississippi Lead Mines. The people in this country have got over their fears of the Indians, but when they go from the wild marches of the enemy and leave the bloody fields, to again seek retirement in their humble cottages, where industry of a growing family had treasured up enough to satisfy all their desires and make their home their earthly heaven, lo! For a distance of 200 miles, not a farmer has been able to raise a bushel of grain. Under all these causes of alarm, every man appears willing to again enter the field, should his services be found necessary and seek revenge of those who caused his misery.*

PRAIRIE DU CHIEN-AREA SITES AND MUSEUMS

Prairie du Chien is the center of many annual gathering and historical reenactment events. Since 1976, the Prairie Villa Rendezvous has been held for individuals interested in experiencing life on the frontier before 1840. Groups also congregate to stage military drills that reference the War of 1812 between British, American and First Nation peoples. The city is across the river from Effigy Mound National Parks and is home to the Wisconsin State Historical Site, Villa Louis and the Fort Crawford Museum.

Reconstructed blockhouse at the site of the first Fort Crawford on St. Feriole Island. Prairie du Chien, Wisconsin.

George Catlin, the American Indian agent and noted painter who documented his interactions with First Nations in his works, captured images of communities engaging in sport, commerce and political negotiations at Prairie du Chien. His painting of girls playing lacrosse resembles the competition of modern softball and baseball leagues that congregate in the summer.

VILLA LOUIS, WISCONSIN STATE HISTORICAL SITE
St. Feriole Island, situated in the middle of the Mississippi off the shores of Prairie du Chien, is an important historic and archaeologically sensitive area. The Wisconsin State Historical Society is revitalizing a series of frontier-era buildings. The island is prone to flooding, so the welcome center has been raised onto stilts. Reenactors provide guided tours of the fur trading and pioneer life of European settlement. The main attraction, Villa Louis, is an impressive estate built onto a large Native American mound.

The first Fort Armstrong was constructed on the grounds of this site. A portion of the fort, a "blockhouse" used for defensive protection, has been rebuilt.

Villa Louis, Wisconsin Historic Site on St. Feriole Island. Prairie du Chien, Wisconsin.

521 Villa Louis Road
P.O. Box 65
Prairie du Chien, WI, 53821-0065
villalouis.wisconsinhistory.org

———

FORT CRAWFORD MUSEUM: PRAIRIE DU CHIEN HISTORICAL SOCIETY
In 1832, Zachary Taylor was tasked with building a new Fort Crawford that would be more suitable to sustain any attacks. The inland fort would serve as the new base of military operations in the area. The stockade was used to contain Black Hawk and the Prophet following their surrender. The museum and tour is open from May through October. A small fee for admittance is charged.

717 South Beaumont Road
Prairie du Chien, WI, 53821
fortcrawfordmuseum.com

Right: Site of second Fort Crawford historic sign. Prairie du Chien, Wisconsin.

Below: Fort Crawford Museum welcome sign. Prairie du Chien, Wisconsin.

MISSISSIPPI RIVER SCULPTURE PARK
Bronze sculptures by Florence Bird capture the spirit of notable figures from Prairie du Chien's past. The free park encourages guests to stroll alongside the realistic and striking interpretation of Black Hawk, Emma Big Bear, a French *voyageur* and others. The park is located a few blocks away from Villa Louis. Admission is free.

191 West Blackhawk Avenue
Prairie du Chien, WI, 53821
statuepark.org

BLACK HAWKIANA AND
BLACK HAWK'S TOUR OF AMERICA

BLACK HAWK PURCHASE. The part of Wisconsin Territory known as the Black Hawk purchase is certainly not exaggerated when it is called the Galaxy of the New World. Throughout the Purchase there seems to have been an evident design in the proportionate distribution of prairie, timber, rock and water. The prairies, tho' more broken than in Illinois, are not at all inaccessible to an easy as well as most pleasant cultivation. How great has the universal architect favored this country.
—Sangamo Journal, *July 9, 1836*

BLACK HAWK ARRIVES IN CLEVELAND. Thousands of our people rushed to the river upon the arrival of one of the lions of the day. The crowd was so uproarious that more than an hour was consumed in attempting to affect a landing. Black Hawk was smuggled ashore.
—Albany Journal, *June 29, 1833*

The Administration prints have become marvelously hostile to Black Hawk. The "green eyed monster" jealousy has taken hold of them. Poor Black Hawk is not to blame that the multitude followed, shouted, huzzaed, and threw up their caps at him *as well as Gen Jackson. It is not* his *fault that the public should have divided in their choice of the* sights *and that some* would *think him the greatest lion of the two. And yet, he is scolded like a very drab, and sent off in a pet to his own people before his tour was half over.*
—Phoenix Gazette, *Alexandria, July 2, 1833*

The public's interest in Black Hawk increased during his imprisonment and forced tour of major cities in the eastern United States. It is unlikely that his American captors knew that the tour would incite what the *Newburgh Telegraph* dubbed "Black Hawkiana." The fervent interest of the locals to view Black Hawk, his son and the other prisoners caused large unruly crowds where "shins were broken—children ran over, and left screaming in the gutters, horses frightened and carts upset…at the eager curiosity."

During the tour of eastern cities, Black Hawk met President Andrew Jackson face to face. Black Hawk noted in his autobiography that Jackson "said he wished to know the *cause* of my going to war against his white children. I thought he ought to have known this before; and, consequently, said but little to him about it—as I expected he knew as well as I could tell him."

For about six weeks, Black Hawk and his compatriots were imprisoned at Fort Monroe. Following Black Hawk's imprisonment and forced parade through major American cities on the East Coast, Black Hawk was finally allowed to return to the Rock Island. The Sauk and Fox tribes were compelled to sign additional treaties that further impinged on their territory. Each of the other Native American tribes in the region, regardless of role in the conflict, would in their own turn be confronted by an American government interested in solely controlling Native American land and resources.

The Indian removal policy of the United States continued after the conclusion of the Black Hawk War. After the war, the Dakotas, a longtime enemy of the Sauk and Fox and who were routinely and strategically set against one another by American forces, now became a focus of removal by the American government. Over the next decades, the same tactics of broken treaties, promises of mutually beneficial trade and encroachment of traditional lands would affect the Dakotas west of the Mississippi.

The Potawatomi Nation in Illinois and Wisconsin, as well as the Ho-Chunks (Winnebagos), would also be forced to sign treaties and surrender the majority of their land. The August 29, 1832 *Galenian* generally summarized the sentiment of Americans: "We are all waiting with great anxiety to learn what will be done at the treaty; and whether the Winnebagoes will be permitted to go unpunished for their traitorous conduct during the war. Nothing can give us any assurance of peace except an entire extinguishment of all the Indian title to the land this side of the lake."

All the First Nations who were either suspected of assisting the British Band or who overtly assisted American troops would eventually be forced to sign new treaties that greatly reduced their control of their traditional lands. Many of the entire communities were forcibly moved to the West or

Black Hawk Ginger Ale label.

South. During Abraham Lincoln's presidency, the policy of Indian removal would continue while the tribulations that would lead to the Civil War took precedence. Winfield Scott would continue to play a role as the military's key enforcer and strategic operator in enforcing the Indian removal policy.

The public interest in Black Hawk's life didn't end after the resolution of the Black Hawk War. The genre of autobiographies of public figures was a ripe and lucrative market. The sentiments in Black Hawk's autobiography should be considered an important firsthand account of the standpoint of American Indians, who faced displacement and persecution at the hands of the U.S. government. Black Hawk's autobiography is one of the few personal accounts of the period that is still being printed. Remembrances by Winfield Scott, Governor Reynolds and others didn't have the appeal, honesty and emotional connection that Black Hawk's autobiography achieved. Copies of his work and the others are out of copyright and can be viewed online for free. It is a remarkable piece of documentation of the era, not only because it is one of the earliest firsthand accounts of the Native American experience of the time but because of how compelling and true the words still ring today.

Antoine Le Clair, U.S. interpreter for the Sauk and Fox, noted:

INDIAN AGENCY, ROCK ISLAND, October 16, 1833. I do hereby certify, that Makataimeshekiakiak, or Black Hawk, did call upon me, on his return to his people in August last, and expressed a great desire to have a History of his Life written and published, in order (as he said) "that the people of the United States, (among whom he had been traveling, and by whom he had been treated with great respect, friendship and hospitality), might know the cause that had impelled him to acts as he had done, and the principles by which he was governed."

The land that Black Hawk and his British Band fought for became part of the United States and was sold off to citizens and speculators. George Davenport utilized his knowledge of the Sauk and Fox lands to purchase a large swath of their territory, including Rock Island. Davenport's early land speculation helped him to become one of the wealthiest people in the region. On the Fourth of July 1845, a group of outlaws, dubbed the "Banditti of the Prairie," robbed and murdered Davenport in his home on Rock Island.

John Kinzie, the Indian agent who worked to keep the Winnebagos out of the conflict, left his position and his newly built Indian Agency House shortly after the war. He would become a major landowner, speculator and political force in the then burgeoning village of Chicago.

Black Hawk's name and image have been adopted by a cacophony of corporations. His name or image has been used to sell or promote corn shellers, golf clubs, socket wrenches, piston grips, bicycles, boots, fly swatters, restaurants, banks, technical colleges, hotels, motels, ginger ale, ginger beer, beer, a film production company, fishing hooks, fishing reels, military helicopters, cars, U.S. naval boats, plays, books and travel guides. His name has been adopted by sports teams from high schools, higher educational institutions and professional hockey.

Within the lifetime of the American veterans who participated in the war, Black Hawk's memory was romanticized by American culture. The play *Black Hawk or Lily of the Valley* by Elizabeth Farnsworth Mears (1830–1907), who adopted the penname Nellie Wildwood, was wildly successful. The opening night crowd in Madison, Wisconsin, was standing room only. Mears's plot included a fictionalized story of a daughter of Black Hawk who assists in saving Alice Hall. The drama ran for three weeks and featured white actors and actresses dawning headdresses and approximations of Native American dress. Elizabeth's daughter, Helen Farnsworth Mears, would become a noted sculptor and was active in Lorado Taft's circle.

The landscape along the western Wisconsin riverway would become inspiration for America's most famous architect, Frank Lloyd Wright. He wrote in his autobiography how the land of Wisconsin and the topography of the rolling hills, the meandering river valleys and ephemeral springs led him to his passion to build.

Wright shared the story of his pioneer forefathers who built their livelihood in the lower Mississippi Valley near today's Spring Green, Wisconsin, and a few miles from the frontier town of Helena. His famous architectural triumph, Taliesin ("Shining Brow" in Welsh), incorporated the living landscape into his building philosophy. His grandfathers immigrated to "the Valley," and the prairie was broken for cropland when "friendly Indians still lingered in the neighborhood." At today's welcome center for Taliesin, the Frank Lloyd Wright Visitors' Center, a small plaque just off the parking lot notes that American soldiers and militia forces passed across the river near the building during the Black Hawk War.

Dodgeville's Edna Meudt (1906–1989), a noted regional poet, grew up on a family farm that encompassed a portion of Dodge's original homestead. Edna "picked watercress in [Dodge's] old creek" and knew of the "Indian marker-maples" in the area. For Dodgeville's bicentennial celebrations in 1976, she wrote a play, *The Promised Land: The Life and Times of Henry Dodge, First Territorial of the State of Wisconsin*. The play focuses on Dodge's later life, as his wife and children review the tribulations of his pioneer days. The play is bookended with a monologue by Dodge's wife, Christina, who notes the lack of women's representation in the histories of the Northwest Territory. In the climax of the action, Dodge's friends—the newspaperman Philleo and Strong, the local banker—discuss the Black Hawk War. Both friends are aghast over the cruelty and bloodthirstiness of American soldiers during the Battle of the Bad Axe River.

Dodge's old homestead and mining camp, which at one time employed more than one hundred settlers, is mostly woodland and farmland. His claim is now marked with a stone plaque down a serene, tree-lined road a few miles away from the four-lane interstate. A small gravel operation and mobile home park reside up the hill.

Henry Dodge would become the first territorial governor of Wisconsin in 1836 and stewarded the Badger State into the Union in 1848. On July 4, 1836, Dodge's minimalist icon of a bulging arm above a pile of ore and rocks was adopted as the image for the territory seal. A second seal was devised

Above: Black Hawk image taken from George Catlin's portrait on a Black Hawk Hotel plate.

Left: Black Hawk Hotel advertising on a match book.

USS *Black Hawk*, World War I. *From the personal collection of a service member.*

USS *Black Hawk* crew, World War I. *From the personal collection of a service member.*

by members of the territorial government that included a Native American standing next to the Mississippi River among lead bars. This seal included the motto *Civilitas Successitt Barbarum* (roughly, "Civilization Advances Over Barbarism"). Shortly after Wisconsin achieved statehood in 1848, a new image was chosen and still serves as the official seal. This emblem includes numerous symbols of the state's economy. A sailor and miner, topped by a gopher-like badger, stand among the harvest of a Wisconsin cornucopia and a pyramid of lead bars. While Dodge's bicep still remains in the 1848 seal—along with the additions of a plow, anchor and pickaxe—references to Native Americans or the influence their early partnership had in the development of the state have been removed.

Governor Dodge would continue his mining claims in the Dodgeville area. He had the distinction of serving in the U.S. Senate alongside his son, who was elected to represent Iowa.

Black Hawk was allotted a small parcel of land near the Des Moines River. He was interred in a traditional grave that was soon looted. While the remains were eventually held by the Burlington Historical Society, they were ultimately lost when the society's building was consumed by fire in 1855.

On July 6, 1833, the *Sangamon Journal* reported on the farewell speech Black Hawk delivered to Colonel Eustis, the commanding officer, upon his release from Fort Monroe in 1833:

> *Brother; I have come on my own part and in behalf of my companions to bid you farewell. Our great father* [President Andrew Jackson] *has at length been pleased to permit us to return to our hunting grounds. We have buried the tomahawk, and the sound of the rifle will hereafter bring death to the deer and the Buffalo....The memory of your friendship will remain till the Great Spirit says it is time for Black Hawk to sing his death song.*

JEFFERSON FINIS DAVIS AND FORT MONROE, VIRGINIA

Jefferson Davis and Black Hawk would both be imprisoned at Fort Monroe, Virginia. In 1833, Davis served as part of the detail that accompanied Black Hawk's trip to the East Coast. In 1865, Davis would find himself a prisoner of the United States within the same fortress.

William H. Upham (1841–1924) was a volunteer with the Belle City Rifles of Racine, Wisconsin, during the Civil War. His experiences and service during the war propelled him to office as the eighteenth governor of Wisconsin from 1895 to 1897. Early in the Civil War, Upham was shot through the shoulder and reported as killed in action. However, Upham survived his injury and recuperated as a prisoner of war in Confederate territory. While under watch by the Confederate troops, Upham recalled seeing the grizzled Confederate president Jefferson Davis inspect the camp. The tide would turn.

Upham gained his freedom through a prisoner exchange. He met President Lincoln, who was impressed with him and recommended Upham for officer training at West Point. By the conclusion of the Civil War, Upham had become a commissioned officer and was serving as a guard at Fort Monroe.

As the Civil War neared a conclusion, soldiers from a Wisconsin and Michigan regiment captured Jefferson Davis on May 10, 1865, in Georgia. Davis was transported to Fort Monroe to be safely imprisoned as American forces deliberated on the best course to deal with the disgraced leader. Enter William H. Upham of Wisconsin.

In his role at Fort Monroe, Upham would serve as one of the prison guards during Jefferson Davis's two years of imprisonment. Upham built up a rapport with Davis during this time. Following Davis's release, his wife reportedly encouraged him to write down his own autobiography. While Davis did write an account of the brief history of the Confederate States, he died before undertaking his autobiography proper. After his death, Jefferson's wife published a thin account of his exploits that unfortunately does not include any pertinent information on his service during the Black Hawk War.

For two years, Jefferson Davis would remain at Fort Monroe, a prisoner in the complex where Black Hawk, the Prophet and other key members of the Black Hawk War were also held during their tour of American East Coast cities in 1832–33. During the disgraced Confederate president's captivity, he shared stories of his time in the Black Hawk War with William Upham.

The State of Wisconsin Historical Museum holds scrapbooks from Upham's family archives that briefly note of Davis's stories of the old Northwest Territory. Mary Kelly Upham's scrapbook relate a few whispers of the experiences Davis shared with Upham of his service in the Northwest Territory before the Black Hawk War:

> *The room was furnished with an iron bed stand, which is familiar to a great many of us, a table and two chairs. Usually upon the table was a box of tobacco and two pipes and sitting on opposite sides with our feet resting upon the table we could sit and chat until both of us were sleeping. As a companion and a man to talk with, Mr. Davis was very pleasant and social. He was full of remembrances and stories of the army and familiarities with all parts of Wisconsin, having crossed the state twice by train from Green Bay and from Milwaukee to Prairie du Chien. The typography of Wisconsin was more familiar to him than to me who had lived nearly all my life in Wisconsin. He could tell me the meaning of nearly all the Indian names of this locality and gave me stories of West Point, and army life. Never to me did he indulge in any bitterness or reflection upon anyone. Political topics were never touched between us, and I presume if they had been we should have been in immediate disagreement.*

Mary Kelly's remembrances are somewhat off-kilter, as there was no train service across Wisconsin during Davis's time in Wisconsin. But it is striking that Davis had a ready knowledge of the Old Northwest's landscape and First Nations in the area.

Jefferson Davis, Abraham Lincoln and the Summer White House in Washington, D.C.

While Abraham Lincoln and Jefferson Davis did not formally meet during their service in the Black Hawk War, their lives would intertwine before they were to meet as adversaries during the Civil War.

Both men would serve in the U.S. Congress during the twenty-ninth session (1847–49). Lincoln was elected to his first term in the House of Representatives from the state of Illinois, and Jefferson Davis was elected to the Senate to represent the state of Mississippi after being appointed to the seat the year before to fill a vacancy. Coincidentally, fellow Black Hawk War veteran Henry Dodge was also in the Senate as the one of the first senators from the brand-new state of Wisconsin. Moreover, Dodge's son, Augustus, also served that term in the same body as the senator for Iowa.

One topic that both Lincoln and Davis tackled as politicians during this term was the care, rehabilitation and housing needs of U.S. veterans. Davis was assigned to the Committee on Military Affairs in the Senate, and Lincoln served on the House side on the Committee on Expenditures in the War Department.

A spending bill during this session would provide for the support of military veterans who had served for twenty years or who had "suffered by reason or disease or wounds incurred in the service and in the line of duty." The expenditure would be specifically earmarked through a bill championed by Jefferson Davis and passed in 1851 that would lead to the construction of the Soldiers' Home in Washington, D.C. The facility continues today as a care center for American veterans.

The cottage on the grounds of the Soldiers' Home for convalescing soldiers would become the informal presidential "summer home." Situated away from the swampland of the interior of Washington, D.C., where the Capitol and White House resided, the Soldiers' Home sat high above the city but in view of the growing metropolis. The setting allowed Lincoln a reprieve from the city and allowed him to speak directly with recuperating soldiers. Lincoln likely wrote most of the Emancipation Proclamation at the cottage. Lincoln visited the Soldiers' Home via horseback on April 13, 1865, the day before he was assassinated.

WASHINGTON, D.C., AND FORT MONROE, VIRGINIA
SITES AND RESOURCES

PRESIDENT LINCOLN'S COTTAGE AT THE SOLDIERS' HOME
Outside of downtown Washington, D.C., and a bit distant from the Metro, President Lincoln's Cottage provides a glimpse into the respite Lincoln sought from the metropolis. With sweeping views of the capital, the expert tours and displays provide a glimpse into a lesser-known part of Lincoln's personal life. The home is a National Historic Landmark and is recognized by the National Trust for Historic Preservation.

140 Rock Creek Church Road, NW
Washington, D.C., 20011
lincolncottage.org

———

NATIONAL MUSEUM OF THE AMERICAN INDIAN
Created with the inspiration, guidance and spirit of First Nations, the National Museum of the American Indian is actively sharing the stories, culture and importance of American Indians. Situated on the National Mall, the museum continues to build critical exhibitions and interpretations that are used in classrooms across the country and beyond.

National Mall
Fourth Street and Independence Avenue, SW
Washington, D.C., 20560
americanindian.si.edu

———

FORT MONROE
41 Bernard Road (Building no. 17, Lee's Quarters)
Fort Monroe, VA, 23651-1001
(757) 722-FORT (3678)
nps.gov

Right: St. Feriole Island Park. Baseball field in Prairie du Chien, Wisconsin.

Below: Ball-play of the Women, Prairie du Chien, George Catlin, 1835–36. *Smithsonian American Art Museum, Gift of Mrs. Joseph Harrison Jr., object no. 1985.66.430.*

This afternoon they had a great game of the cross [lacrosse] *on the prairie* [Prairie du Chien], *between the Sious* [Dakotas] *on the one side, and the Puants and Reynards* [Sauk and Fox] *on the other. The ball is made of some hard substance and covered with leather; the cross-sticks are round and net-work, with handles three feet long. The parties being ready, and bets agreed upon, sometimes the amount of some thousand dollars, the goals are set up on the prairie at the distance of half a mile. The ball is thrown up in the middle, and each party strives to drive it to the opposite goal; when either party gains the first rubber, which*

is driving quick around the post, the ball is again taken to the center, the ground changed, and the contest renewed; and this is continued until one side gains four times, which decides the bet. It is an interesting sight to see two or three hundred naked savages contending on the plain who shall bear off the palm of victory; as he who drives the ball is much shouted at by his companions.

From The Expeditions of Zebulon Montgomery Pike (1779–1813), *vol. 1.*

Northwest Territory 1832

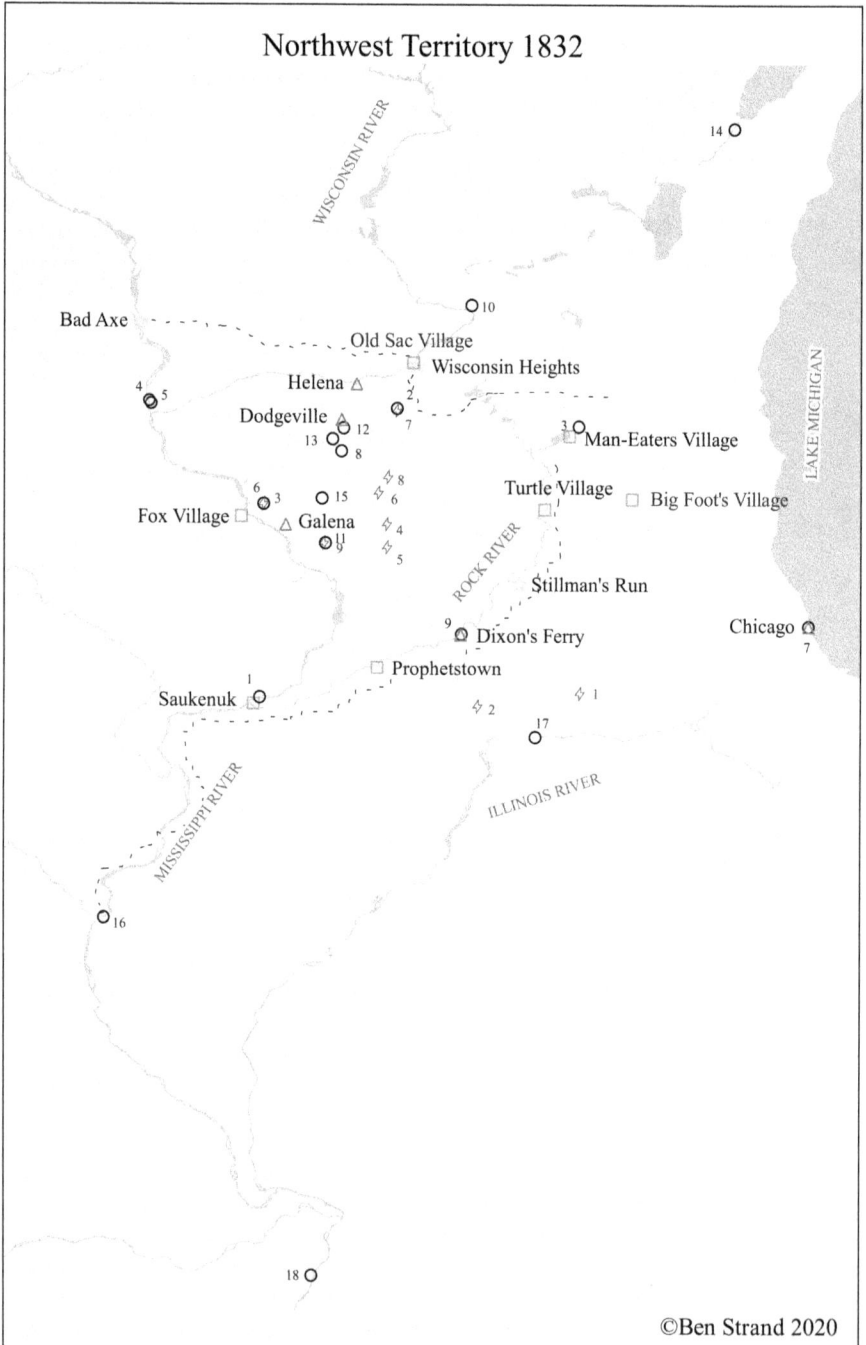

WISCONSIN RIVER

14 O

O 10

Bad Axe

Old Sac Village

□ Wisconsin Heights

Helena △

4
O 5

Dodgeville △

13 O 12

O 8

O 7

3 O
□ Man-Eaters Village

6
O 3

O 15

⚡ 8

⚡ 6

Turtle Village
□

□ Big Foot's Village

Fox Village □

△ Galena

⚡ 4

O 11
9

⚡ 5

ROCK RIVER

Stillman's Run

9
O
Dixon's Ferry

Chicago O
7

□ Prophetstown

1
Saukenuk O

⚡ 2

⚡ 1

17
O

ILLINOIS RIVER

LAKE MICHIGAN

MISSISSIPPI RIVER

16 O

18 O

©Ben Strand 2020

Appendix A
BATTLEFIELDS, AMERICAN INDIAN COMMUNITIES, VILLAGES, FORTS

SYMBOL	SITE
☐	American Indian Community
▲	American Village
★	Major Battle
⚡	Skirmish
1	Indian Creek Massacre
2	Ament's Cabin
3	Sinisnawa Mound Raid
4	Waddam's Grove
5	Kellogg's Grove
6	Spafford Farm Attack
7	Blue Mounds Fort Raid
8	Battle of the Pecatonica
9	Apple River Fort Raid

SYMBOL	SITE
◯	American Fort
1	Fort Armstrong
2	Fort Bingham
3	Fort Koshkonong
4	Fort Crawford
5	Fort Crawford Rebuilt
6	Fort Sinsinawa
7	Fort Dearborn
8	Fort Defiance
9	Fort Dixon
10	Fort Winnebago
11	Apple River Fort
12	Fort Union
13	Fort Jackson
14	Fort Howard
15	Fort Gratiot
16	Fort Johnson
17	Fort Wilbourn

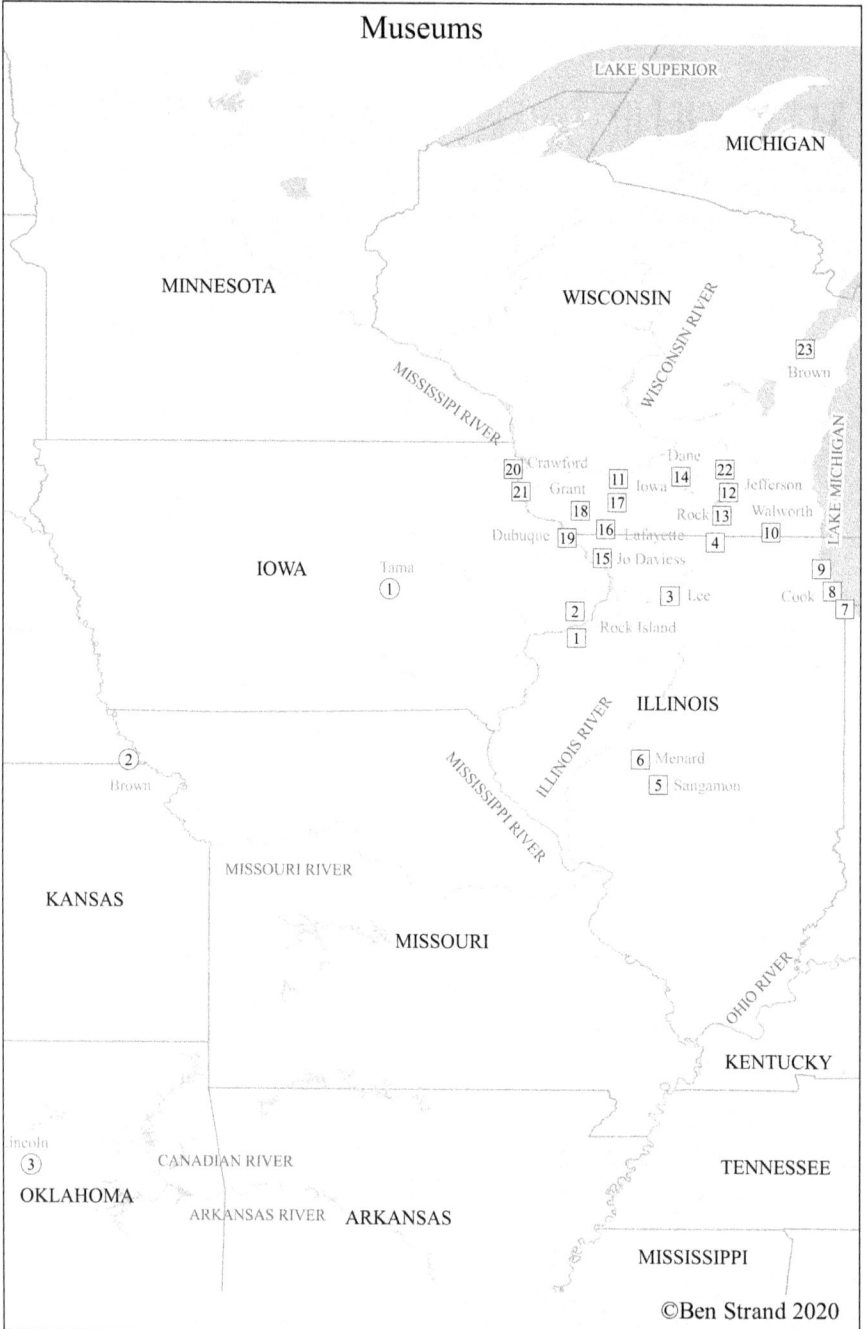

Museums

LAKE SUPERIOR

MICHIGAN

MINNESOTA

WISCONSIN

WISCONSIN RIVER

MISSISSIPI RIVER

[23]
Brown

LAKE MICHIGAN

Crawford
Dane
[20]
[21] Grant
[18]
[11] Iowa
[17]
[14]
[22]
[12] Jefferson
Rock [13]
Walworth
[10]
Dubuque [19]
[16] Lafayette
[4]
[15] Jo Daviess

IOWA
Tama
①

[3] Lee

[9]
Cook [8]
[7]

[2]
[1] Rock Island

ILLINOIS

ILLINOIS RIVER

MISSISSIPPI RIVER

②
Brown

[6] Menard
[5] Sangamon

MISSOURI RIVER

KANSAS

MISSOURI

KENTUCKY

OHIO RIVER

Lincoln
③
OKLAHOMA

CANADIAN RIVER

TENNESSEE

ARKANSAS RIVER   ARKANSAS

MISSISSIPPI

Appendix B
MUSEUMS, PARKS AND HISTORIC SITES

○

1. Meskwaki Cultural Center and Museum
2. Museum of the Sac and Fox Nation of Missouri in Kansas and Nebraska
3. Sac and Fox National Public Library

☐

1. John Hauberg Indian Museum
2. The Arsenal Historical Society
3. Northwest Territory Historic Center
4. Logan Museum of Anthropology
5. Abraham Lincoln Presidential Library and Museum
6. Lincoln's New Salem State Historic Site
7. Newberry Library
8. Chicago History Museum
9. Mitchell Museum of the American Indian
10. Geneva Lake Museum
11. Iowa County Historical Society
12. Hoard Historical Museum
13. Milton House Museum
14. Wisconsin Historical Museum
15. Apple River Fort State Historic Site
16. Shullsburg Badger Mine and Museum
17. Pendarvis (Wisconsin Historical Society)
18. The Mining Museum and Rollo Jamison Museum
19. The National Mississippi River Museum and Aquarium
20. Fort Crawford Museum—Prairie du Chien Historical Society
21. Villa Louis, Wisconsin State Historical Site
22. Vernon County Historical Society
23. Heritage Hill State Park

Appendix C
BLACK HAWK WAR TIMELINES

1634	Jean Nicolet, a French explorer, founds a trading post near present-day Green Bay.
1693	French traders establish post on Madeleine Island in Lake Superior.
1701–2	French and Fox Wars.
1716	Mississippi Bubble, a French financial crisis over speculation of land claims in North America.
1767	Approximate birth year of Black Hawk.
1796	Spanish Mines. Julien Dubuque receives permission from the Spanish Crown to continue mining near present-day Dubuque in partnership with Meskwaki Tribe.
1803	Fort Dearborn is built in Chicago.
1804	Disputed treaty that cedes all Sauk and Fox lands east of the Mississippi. From Black Hawk's autobiography: "It has been the origin of all our serious difficulties with the whites....After questioning Quashquame about the sale of our lands, he assured me that he 'never had consented to the sale.'"
	Meriwether Lewis and William Clark Expedition to the Pacific Ocean departs north of St. Louis.
1807	U.S. Congress approves Northwest Territory for mining licenses.
1808	United States government builds Fort Madison at the mouth of the Des Moines River, on the Mississippi. The Sauk and American Indian communities disapprove of the presence of the settlement.
1812	War between the British and United States. Black Hawk and many Sauk and Fox members align with Tecumseh and the British. Black Hawk participates in raids on the Mississippi River.

Fort Dearborn in Chicago is burned down by Potawatomi forces. John Kinzie is taken prisoner and later released. Fort Shelby is built by American forces on St. Feriole Island adjacent to Prairie du Chien.

1813   Fort Madison is abandoned by retreating American forces.

1814   Battle of Rock Island Rapids, or the Battle of Campbell Island, July 19. Black Hawk leads a force of perhaps five hundred Sauk and Fox and defeats U.S. forces led by Lieutenant John Campbell. British forces conquer Fort Shelby and rename it Fort McKay.

1815   Americans and British sign a treaty to end the war.

1816   American forces rebuild Fort McKay on St. Feriole Island and name it Fort Crawford.

Fort Armstrong is built on Rock Island (now called Arsenal Island) near Saukenuk.

1822   Two Kentuckians are awarded the first mining licenses to operate on the Fever River in Illinois.

William Clark is named superintendent of Indian affairs.

1827   Winnebago War. Red Bird attacks settlers near first Fort Crawford, in Prairie du Chien.

1828   The *Miner's Journal* begins publication in Galena, Illinois.

1829   Glut of lead production in the Northwest Territory.

1830   The Indian Removal Act is authorized by Congress and signed into law by President Andrew Jackson.

1831   Alexis de Tocqueville travels America to research the prison system. His impressions will be published in 1835 in *Democracy in America*.

TIMELINE FOCUS, 1831–1833

1831

April 30   Rock River citizens petition Illinois governor John Reynolds to remove the Sauk and Fox, who have returned to summer residency on Saukenuk.

June 4–7   Major General Gaines meets with leaders of the "British Band of Sauks" regarding the treaty of 1804. A Sauk woman stands and addresses Gaines, stating that the women had cultivated the land and they had never sold the land.

June 25   General Gaines openly assembles a large force of Illinois militia, two regiments of federal troops and a steamboat at Fort Armstrong.

June 30   Articles of Agreement and Capitulation are signed by Governor Reynolds, General Gaines and thirty chiefs and braves. The document is not signed by Black Hawk or the Prophet.

July   Sauk and Fox members attack a group of Menomonees near
            Prairie du Chien in retaliation for prior violence committed by
            the Menomonees.
Sept 5   Council at Fort Armstrong with Indian agent Felix St. Vrain
            and leaders of the Sauk and Fox regarding the attack on the
            Menomonees. Keokuk noted, "What they did [Menominees]
            and what we did, was put in Scales the balance."

1832

April 5–6   Black Hawk's "British Band" crosses the Mississippi by the Yellow
            Banks.
April 13   General Atkinson holds a council with Keokuk, Wapello and
            other chiefs from the Sauk and Fox tribes who remained west of
            the Mississippi and were not part of the British Band.
May 5   U.S. Congress passes Indian Inoculation Act to confront smallpox
            outbreaks.
May 11   Prophetstown is incinerated by General Whiteside. The Prophet's
            followers and the British Band had already moved farther east
            along the Rock River.
May 14   Battle of Stillman's Run.
May 19   William Durley is ambushed near Polo, Illinois.
May 21   Indian Creek Massacre, near Ottawa, Illinois. Sylvia and Rachel
            Hall are taken prisoner, and fifteen settlers are killed. The
            aggressors were not part of the British Band.
May 26   General Dodge convenes council at Four Lakes with Winnebagos
            to request assistance.
June 1   Rachel and Sylvia Hall are released at Fort Bluc Mounds.
June 15   First battle at Kellogg's Grove, Illinois. Indian agent Felix St.
            Vrain and three militia soldiers are killed.
June 16   Battle of the Pecatonica, or Horse Shoe Bend, near Hamilton's
            Diggings, Wiota, Wisconsin.
June 20   Blue Mounds Fort attack.
June 24   Apple River Fort is attacked by Black Hawk, Elizabeth, Illinois.
June 25   Second battle at Kellogg's Grove, Illinois. Captain Dement's
            militia was confronted by Black Hawk and warriors from the
            British Band.
June 28   General Winfield Scott departs Buffalo, New York, with four ships.
June 29   Sinisnawa Mound Raid.
June 30   General Scott reaches Detroit. Scott writes to Atkinson, noting
            that he will have a force of 950 men, two six-pounders and one
            howitzer and should be in Chicago by July 9.

July 10   Winfield Scott's steamer, the *Sheldon Thompson*, arrives in Chicago. American troops are waylaid by cholera and unable to proceed.

July 16   George Harrison and Abraham Lincoln are discharged from the militia at Cold Spring, Wisconsin.

July 17   Atkinson receives news about cholera infecting Winfield Scott's troops in Chicago.

July 18   Black Hawk Band crosses the Four Lakes region, today's Madison, Wisconsin, and UW–Madison campus.

July 19   Battle of Wisconsin Heights.

July 28   Dodge and Atkinson's forces cross the Wisconsin River at Helena.

Aug 2   Black Hawk attempts to surrender to the crew of the *Warrior* and is fired upon.

Aug 3   Massacre at the Battle of Bad Axe.

Aug 27   Black Hawk surrenders to Colonel Zachary Taylor and General Joseph Street at Fort Armstrong, Prairie du Chien.

Sept 13   Winnebagos sign treaty ceding their land south and east of the Wisconsin River and surrendering eight men involved in raids on settlers.

1833

April 25   General Andrew Jackson and Black Hawk meet in Washington, D.C.

April 26   Black Hawk arrives at Fort Monroe, and his imprisonment begins.

June 6   Black Hawk's forced tour of East Coast cities.

June 12   Black Hawk arrives in New York City.

August 2   Black Hawk returns to Fort Armstrong on Rock Island and is released.

AFTERMATH OF THE BLACK HAWK WAR

1833   Chicago Treaty is signed by the Potawatomis. The nation cedes their lands east of the Mississippi River, Chief Big Foot and the Potawatomi Nation are forced to leave village on Geneva Lake.

1834   *Life of Makataimeshekiakiak, or Black Hawk, Embracing the Traditions of His Nation* is published.

           Colonel George Davenport finishes his home on Rock Island. He had received the land as part of the new treaty in compensation for his claims against the British Band.

           End of government control of lead mines. Public land sales and auctions begin in Mineral Point.

1837   Black Hawk joins Keokuk, and members of the Sauk, Fox and Ioway, for a tour of eastern cities to promote George Catlin's "Indian Gallery." These sold-out lectures allowed Americans to see First Nation people in person. The talks featured Catlin's portraits and his interpretations of the traditions of American Indians.

1838   Black Hawk dies in Iowa on October 3.

1840   Forced Ho-Chunk (Winnebago) removal is attempted. General Atkinson leads the effort to move members of the tribe to Iowa.

1846   Iowa statehood achieved.

1847   Keokuk dies in the Kansas land of the Sauk and Fox.

1848   California Gold Rush begins. Many miners in the Lead Mine Region abandon their claims for California.

Wisconsin statehood achieved.

1849   Zachary Taylor, veteran of Black Hawk War, is elected president of the United States; he dies in office the following year.

1850   William Hamilton, son of Alexander Hamilton, dies in California pursuing gold mine claims.

1857   Meskwaki Settlement is founded in Iowa.

Black Hawk, or Lily of the Prairie, a play by Nellie Wildwood, debuts on February 28 in Madison, Wisconsin.

1858   Lincoln delivers his "House Divided" speech in Springfield, Illinois.

1859   Lincoln visits Milwaukee, Wisconsin, to address the Agricultural Society; he visits Tallman home in Janesville, Wisconsin.

Shabbona's death.

1860   On November 6, Abraham Lincoln is elected president, with Hannibal Hamlin as his vice president.

Hannibal Hamlin Garland is born in West Salem, Wisconsin, thirty miles north of Bad Axe River.

1861   On April 12, commander of Fort Sumpter and Black Hawk War veteran Robert Anderson surrenders the fortress to Confederate troops after three days of bombardment.

In October, Winfield Scott, general-in-chief, retires after his Anaconda Plan fails to succeed.

1862   USS *Black Hawk* is commissioned and serves Union troops in the Mississippi Squadron during the Civil War.

1862   Dakota (Sioux) war in Minnesota. President Lincoln orders release of 264 Dakotas and approves the hanging of 38 Dakotas at Mankato, Minnesota.

1865   On April 15, President Lincoln is assassinated in Washington, D.C.

1866   Confederate president Jefferson Davis (1808–1889) is imprisoned at Fort Monroe. He will be released in 1868.

1867   Death of Henry Dodge in Iowa.

1868   Birth of Edward Curtis, the "Dream Catcher," in Cold Spring, Wisconsin. Curtis would dedicate his life to photographing Native American people and cultural traditions.

1887   Kellogg's Grove Monument is dedicated near Kent, Illinois.

1891   First of three Black Hawk's Watch Towers in Rock Island is constructed, with a community amusement park and theaters, overlooking Arsenal Island. Site of current Black Hawk State Park.

1892   Black Hawk statue is erected in Spencer Square, Rock Island, Illinois, on November 28, donated by O.J. Dimick.

1893   Antonin Dvorak (1841–1904) spends the summer in Spillville, Iowa, and meets area First Nation tribal members. His *New World Symphony* is first performed later that year.

1897   Julien Dubuque monument is erected at Spanish Mines near Dubuque, Iowa.

1901   Battle Ground Memorial Park, Stillman Valley, Illinois, is dedication on July 11.

1911   *The Eternal Indian* by Lorado Taft, also referred to as the "Black Hawk" statue, is unveiled on the Rock River outside Oregon, Illinois.

1914   The general public is welcomed at the powwow at Meskwaki Settlement.

1916   The centennial of Fort Armstrong is celebrated in Rock Island, Illinois.

1926   The Chicago Hockey Club's inaugural season as the Black Hawks begins.

1932   The State of Illinois Historical Society publishes a centennial edition of sites and the general progression of the Black Hawk War.

1934   The statue of Chief Black Hawk by Harry E. Stinson is dedicated in Lake View, Iowa.

1940   Meskwakis perform a powwow near Saukenuk at Black Hawk Historic Site, Rock Island, Illinois.

1942   Black Hawk State Park, CCC Watch Tower Lodge in Rock Island, Illinois, opens with guests including Mary Mack, great-great-granddaughter of Black Hawk. The statue of Black Hawk is moved from Spencer Square to the front of the lodge.

1946   The Tri-Cities Blackhawks basketball team is established in Moline, Illinois. The club is still part of the National Basketball Association under the name the Atlanta Hawks.

1948   Governor Dodge State Park is founded outside Dodgeville, Wisconsin. The park has grown from 160 acres to 5,260 acres as of 2019.

1953	American Indian Center Inc. (AIC) is founded in Chicago.
1971	First "Black Hawk Pageant" to unveil the reconstructed Fort Cosconong in Fort Atkinson, Wisconsin, takes place.
1976	U.S. Bicentennial. Dodgeville, Wisconsin poet Edna Meudt debuts the play *Promised Land, The Life and Times of Henry Dodge, First Territorial Governor of Wisconsin.*
	Mesquakie and Proud of It is published.
1990	The State of Wisconsin formally apologizes to the Sauk and Fox Nations at a ceremony at the Battle of the Bad Axe via Wisconsin Assembly Resolution.
	Native American Graves Protection and Repatriation Act (NAGPRA) sets guidelines to protect Native American burial sites and cultural material, as well as establish rules to return remains and objects when possible to associated communities.
1993	The Black Hawk mural in Rock Island, Illinois, is completed by Wisconsinite Richard Haas.
1996	*One Last Glance*, a statue of Chief Bigfoot by Jay Brost, is installed at Reid Park, Fontana, Wisconsin.
2004	The National Museum of the American Indian opens on the National Mall in Washington, D.C.
	Bronze statue of Abraham Lincoln and Black Hawk entitled *Paths of Conviction, Footsteps of Fate* by Jeff Adams is dedicated in Oregon, Illinois.
2006	*Meskwakiinaki Kobetti Nenosoki*, the buffalo that resides in the land of the Meskwakis—buffalo return to the Meskwaki Settlement.
2018	The University of Wisconsin–Madison dedicates a plaque on Bascom Hill recognizing the Ho-Chunk Nation's traditional homeland, including the Four Lakes area.
2019	A Black Hawk mural created by artist Jeff Henriquez is unveiled in downtown Janesville, Wisconsin.

Historic Markers and Plaques

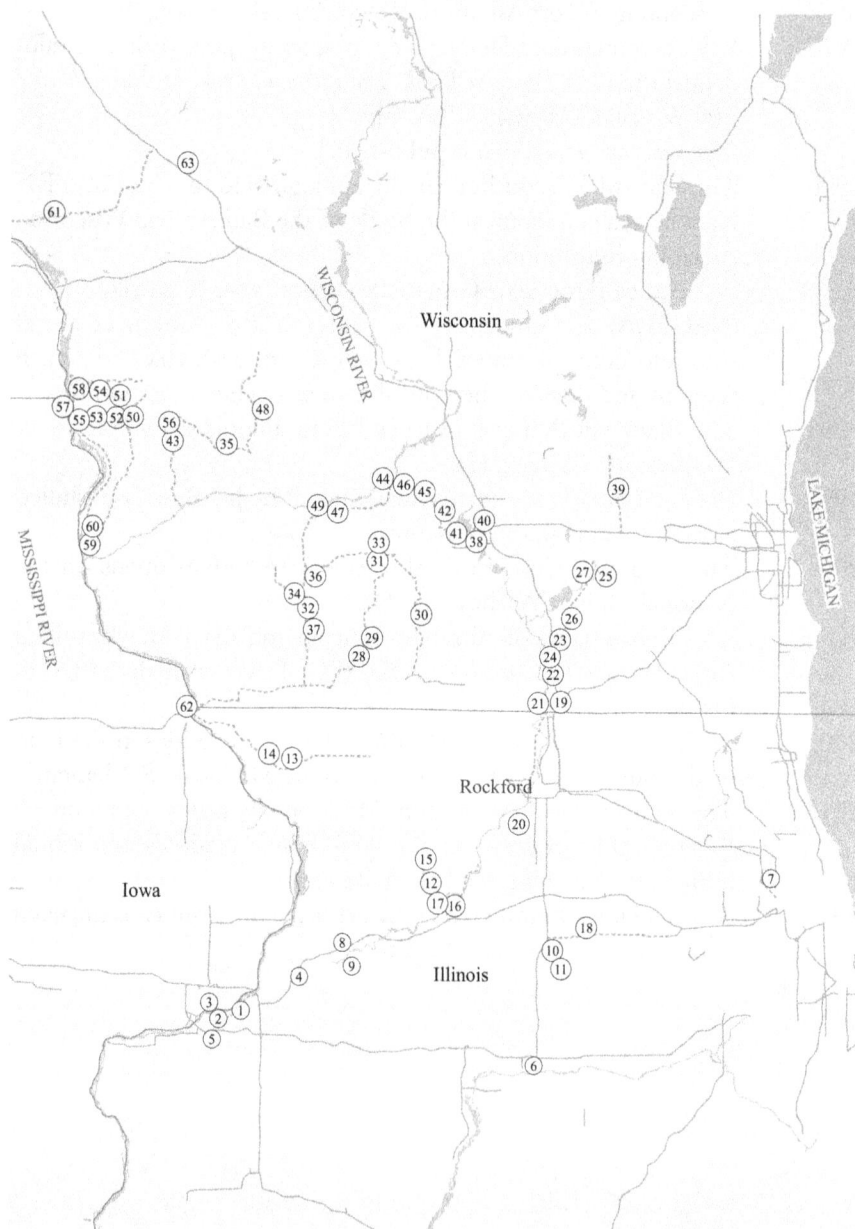

Wisconsin

Rockford

Iowa

Illinois

MISSISSIPPI RIVER

WISCONSIN RIVER

LAKE MICHIGAN

©Ben Strand 2020

Appendix D
HISTORIC MARKERS AND PLAQUES

1. WAR OF 1812. In memory of 10 US Regulars, 4 Illinois Rangers, One Woman and One Child Killed on July 19, 1814 in a Battle between US Soldiers under Lieut. John Campbell, and Sac and Fox Indians under their War Chief Black Hawk. [41.538021, -90.436804]

2. ARSENAL ISLAND. Rock Island, surrounded by the waters of the Mississippi, played a significant part in the opening of the west. The Indians in the area early recognized the strategic advantage of the island and held ceremonial gatherings here. Nearby, at Campbell and Credit Islands, were fought the westernmost campaigns of the War of 1812. Fort Armstrong, at the lower end of Rock Island, was garrisoned from 1816 to 1836, and the Black Hawk War ended here in 1832. Among the troops that served in this vicinity were future presidents Zachary Taylor and Abraham Lincoln. The Island was the home of Indian trader George Davenport. [41.5172, -90.5391]

3. FORT ARMSTRONG. Fort Armstrong was built in 1816–1817. Its riverside was protected by limestone bluffs and its other sides were formed in part by the rear walls of barracks and storehouses. Blockhouses, like the replica, stood at three corners. The pyramid of cannon balls to the southwest marks the site of the northeastern blockhouse. The fort was garrisoned by United States troops until May 4, 1836. It served as headquarters for the Sac and Fox Indian Agent from 1836 to 1838 and as a military depot from 1840 to 1845. It was destroyed by fire in 1855. [41.516716, -90.565614]

4. ROCK ISLAND BRIDGE. In 1832 when Black Hawk and his Sauk and Fox followers returned to Illinois, 1500 mounted volunteers advanced along the bank of the Rock River to capture them. 505 men under Colonel Zachary Taylor followed in supply boats and late at night on May 12, 1832 camped in this area. [41.6024, -90.1677]

5. LINCOLN MILITIA SERVICE. On May 8, 1832, while encamped approximately one mile west of this point, Abraham Lincoln was mustered into the military service of the United States. Captain Lincoln's company was mustered into state service at Beardstown April 28, the day before beginning the march to this place by way of Yellow Banks or Oquawka. [41.442953, -90.568529]

6. FORT WILBORN. On the eminence to the southwest stood Fort Wilbourn. Where the third army of Illinois volunteers was mustered in for service in the Black Hawk War, here on June 16, 1832. Abraham Lincoln enlisted as a private in Jacob M. Early's company, his third enlistment of the war. Erected by the Illinois State Historical Society 1934. [41.311526, -89.088015]

7. ARMY TRAIL ROAD. This road followed an Indian trail that began in Chicago and went through Dupage, Kane, DeKalb, Boone and Winnebago Counties to a Winnebago Village at Beloit, Wisconsin. In August 1832, during the Black Hawk War, United States Army reinforcements from the Eastern Department followed the trail. Their general, Winfield Scott, left Chicago ahead of the troops and took a different route to the war area. Delayed by cholera, his men did not reach the front until after Black Hawk's defeat. The tracks left by heavy army wagons formed a road for early settlers. Erected by the Dupage Chapter Daughters of the American Colonists and The Illinois State Historical Society. 1974. [41.931934, -87.994061]

7.1. PROPHETS TOWN. Prophetstown occupies the site of the village of the Winnebago Prophet, which the Illinois volunteers destroyed on May 10, 1832, in the first act of hostility in the Black Hawk War. [41.6738, -89.9417]

8. WABOKIESHIEK, WHITE CLOUD. The Prophet. Native Americans lived along the lower portion of the Rock River for thousands of years. Through time they were drawn to the area's abundance of fish and wild game and its ability to grow domesticated plants. During the early 1800s the Sauk lived in villages at and near Prophetstown. Wabokieshiek, White Cloud, The Prophet (circa 1790–1841) was an advisor to Black Hawk. This area known

APPENDIX D

as "Prophet's Village" was burned by Captain Abraham Lincoln's Company
during the Black Hawk War. 1832—Black Hawk and Wabokieshiek were
captured in WI. [41.673088, -89.934238]

9. OLD CHICAGO TRAIL. The Old Chicago Trail extended from Fort Dearborn
to Galena. A government mail route was established along this Indian trail
in 1829. The Potawatomi ceded their territory to the government in 1833.
This route became the first East–West stagecoach trail across Northern
Illinois. Paw Paw Grove, one of the first settlements along the route, was a
midway haven between Chicago and Galena. It was over this trail Poetess
Margaret Fuller traveled in 1843, she wrote: "We traveled the blooming
plain unmarked by any road, only the friendly track of the wheels which
beat, not broke the grass. Our stations were not from town to town, but from
grove to grove." [41.688597, -88.981272]

10. PAW PAW GROVE. Deep within the Paw Paw Grove, or As-Sim-In-Eh-
Kon, Potawatomi Chief Waubonsie and his tribe made their home 1824–
1836. At the Treaty of Prairie du Chien 1829, Madeline Ogee, Potawatomi
wife of Joseph Ogee, was granted two sections of land in the granted two
sections of land in the grove. Potawatomi, Chippewa, Ottawa Chiefs,
Waubonsie, Shabbona, and Sauganash (Billy Caldwell) aided the U.S.
Government during the Black Hawk War. At the Treaty of Chicago, 1833,
the Potawatomi Confederation ceded approximately 5 million acres of land
in northwest Illinois to the government. In 1836 the Indians were removed
from their homes to northwest Missouri and southwest Iowa. The Ogee
section was sold to David town for $1,000 in silver. [41.6856, -88.9787]

11. GALENA ROAD. In the early 1830s pioneer traffic moving north from
Peoria crowded primitive trails and forced a direct route to Galena. In
1833, Levi Warner's state survey marked the "Galena Road." It cut through
this schoolyard. Private Abraham Lincoln passed this site June 13, 1832 in
Captain Elijah Iles's Black Hawk War Company. [41.95976, -89.579014]

12. APPLE RIVER FORT. Here, during the Black Hawk War, was located Apple
River Fort, constructed by 45 residents in response to rumors of an Indian
uprising. The 10,000 sq. foot fort with walls 12 feet high contained several
cabins and a two story blockhouse. On June 24, 1832, Black Hawk and
200 warriors attacked while most of the men were out hunting. Elizabeth
Armstrong rallied the women and defenders until relief arrived. Only one

frontiersman, George W. Herlerode, lost his life during the 45 minute battle. In honor of Mrs. Armstrong, the Apple River Settlement was renamed Elizabeth on November 25, 1842. [42.318162, -90.220551]

13. GALENA. Prior to 1820, Indians and occasional white traders occupied LaPointe, the name given to the present site of Galena. The settlement grew rapidly in 1823 and 1824 as each boat deposited new arrivals on the banks of the Fever (now Galena) River. The town was laid out in 1826, and the name changed to Galena (Latin for sulphide of lead). Terror reigned in the region during the Black Hawk War in 1832, but the suppression of the Indians cleared the way for unrestricted white settlement. As supply center for the mines and shipping point for the growing river commerce, Galena became a thriving city when Chicago was still a swamp village. Galena's zenith arrived in the 1840s, and residents lavished money on elaborate houses, many of which still stand today. By the 1850s the surface lead deposits were depleted; the Galena River, once over 300 feet wide, began to gather silt; and the railroads started to take the river commerce. Ulysses S. Grant arrived here in 1860 to work in his father's leather store. A year later this still obscure clerk marched off to the Civil War; in 1865, he returned in triumph to a gift mansion donated by his Galena neighbors. Grant was so prominent that he overshadowed the town's eight other Civil War generals. In 1869, after his election as President of the United States, Grant appointed his Galena friends John A. Rawlins, Secretary of War; Elihu B. Washburne, Secretary of State; Ely S. Parker, Commissioner of Indian Affairs. [42.333352, -90.272083]

14. BUFFALO GROVE. Early in the Black Hawk War Indians concealed near this spot in Buffalo Grove, May 19, 1832, killed William Durley, a member of a six man detail carrying dispatches from Colonel James M. Strode at Galena to General Henry Atkinson at Dixon's Ferry. Durley's body now rests beneath this memorial. [41.990728, -89.602691]

15. LINCOLN IN DIXON. May 12, 1832 Captain Abraham Lincoln's company of Illinois volunteers camped one mile west. Lincoln re-enlisted in two other companies and was frequently in Dixon. Discharged from service near Fort Atkinson, Wisconsin, on July 10, Lincoln passed through Dixon en route to New Salem. [41.838090, -89.468337]

16. Lincoln's Service in Black Hawk War. Abraham Lincoln was stationed here during the Black Hawk War in 1832, as captain of volunteers. On April 21, 1832, he enlisted at Richland Creek, Sangamon County, and was elected captain. He was mustered into state service at Beardstown on April 22 and into United States service at the mouth of Rock River May 3. At the mouth of Fox River on May 27, he was mustered out and on the same day re-enlisted as a private in Captain Elijah Iles' Company. At the expiration of this enlistment, he re-enlisted on June 16, at Fort Wilbourn in Captain Jacob M. Early's Company, and was finally mustered out of service on July 10, 1832, at White Water River, Wisconsin. [41.8464, -89.4852]

17. Shabbona. In the early 1800s Shabbona was a principal chief of the Ottawa, Potawatomi, and Chippewa group of tribes which banded together to form "The Three Fires." Shabbona camped briefly in a large grove one-half mile south of here. He fought with the British in the War of 1812 and later helped the settlers of northern Illinois by warning of Indian uprisings during the Winnebago outbreak. In the Black Hawk War, Shabbona alerted pioneers to impending Indian raids and offered to lead an attack against the Sauk and Fox Tribes. [41.767689, -88.861919]

18. Black Hawk War. In the spring of 1831, the Sauk Indians led by Chief Keokuk left their ancestral home near the mouth of the Rock River and moved across the Mississippi, to fulfill the terms of a treaty signed in 1804. On April 6, 1832, a dissatisfied faction led by Black Hawk returned with 400 warriors and 1200 women, children and old men. Why he risked this retun to "my towns, my cornfields, and the homes of my people" in the face of certain opposition is not clear, but Black Hawk probably hoped that other Indians would join him in resisting further white settlement. When this hope failed and the Illinois militia was called up, Black Hawk sent messengers to negotiate for peaceable removal across the Mississippi. One of his messengers was shot by the excited and poorly-disciplined militia and the war was on. The Indians briefly took the offensive and scalping parties attacked isolated communities of white settlers. The exact route taken by Black Hawk as he retreated through southern Wisconsin toward the Mississippi is difficult to trace, because both pursuers and pursued were traveling unfamiliar terrain and their later accounts varied. Major engagements took place at Wisconsin Heights and at the Bad Axe, where the war ended August 2, 1832. Erected 1968. [42.504848, -88.985182]

19. STILLMAN'S RUN. Here, on May 14, 1832, the first engagement of the Black Hawk War took place, when 275 Illinois militiamen under Maj. Isaiah Stillman were put to flight by Black Hawk and his warriors. So thoroughly demoralized were the volunteers that a new army had to be called into the field. [42.106924, -89.17647]

20. BLACK HAWK AND THE U.S. MILITARY AT TURTLE VILLAGE. Turtle Village, a large and important Ho-Chunk (Winnebago) Indian Village, once stood on the east side of the Rock River near its confluence with Turtle Creek. During the Black Hawk War, the Ho-Chunk sheltered Sac Indian leader Black Hawk and his followers during their northern escape from the military in Illinois. After Black Hawk left Turtle Village, Chief Whirling Thunder ordered the village abandoned, fearing military retaliation. The Ho-Chunk never returned. Erected 1998. In this vicinity, during the Black Hawk War of 1832, Sac Indian leader Black Hawk and his followers left Illinois and entered the Michigan Territory (now Wisconsin), seeking refuge with the Ho-Chunk Indians at Turtle Village. On July 1, 1832 more than five weeks after Black Hawk left Turtle Village and continued his northern retreat up the Rock River, General Henry Atkinson and his troops arrived here, only to find an abandoned Indian settlement with extensive gardens and fields of grain. Erected 1998. [42.50086, -89.034831]

21. ROUTE OF ABRAHAM LINCOLN 1832 AND 1859. Twice in his lifetime Abraham Lincoln is known to have traveled within sight of the Rock River east of this marker. Lincoln passed this way July 2, 1832 as a private in a mounted company of Illinois militia accompanying forces under General Henry Atkinson during the Black Hawk War. On October 1, 1859, Abe Lincoln again passed this way after delivering a political address in Hanchett's Hall at the invitation of the Beloit Republican Club. He spoke the same evening in Janesville and spend the weekend as a guest in the home of William M. Tallman. While following the Prairie Road between Beloit and Janesville in 1859 Lincoln pointed out to this companions the route taken by the army in pursuit of Black Hawk's band. Erected 1960. [42.593967, -89.02215]

22. BLACK HAWK'S GROVE. Black Hawk's Grove. According to local tradition, Black Hawk's band went North up the Rock River, camping several days here at Spring Brook Creek and giving the Hall girls to Winnebago Indians who later ransomed them to settlers. Pursued by General Henry Atkinson's

troops, Black Hawk continued north, then west to cross the Mississippi, but most of the Indians drowned or were killed by troops in August at the Battle of the Bad Axe. Threee years later, Janesville settlers found the remains of Indian tent poles and campfires and called this place Black Hawk's Grove. Erected 2001. [42.674034, -88.994927]

23. THE BLACK HAWK WAR. In April 1832, unhappy about their forced relocation to Iowa and mis-advised by tribal chiefs, about 1,000 Sac, Fox and Kickapoo men, women and children followed Sac war leader Black Hawk back to their homesteads and settlements in Illinois and Michigan territories. At the May 21 Indian Creek raid, 15 settlers were killed and two sisters, the Hall girls captured. Erected 2001. [42.673951, -88.995706]

24. BLACK HAWK WAR ENGAGEMENT "BURNT VILLAGE." A large Ho-Chunk (Winnegabo) Village dating from the 1700s once stood in this vicinity. Just before the 1832 Black Hawk War, the village was burned during an intra-tribal battle. On July 6th and 8th, the United States military camped at this site in their pursuit of Black Hawk and named this place Burnt Village. Erected 1998. [42.914765, -88.779504]

25. STORR'S LAKE. On July 1, 1832, here beside Storrs Lake, Brigadier General Herny Atkinson and 4,500 soldiers camped overnight in their pursuit of Black Hawk. Sac Indian chief, who was fleeing northward up the east side of the Rock River with 400 warriors and 1,200 women and children. In a diary dated, July 1, 1832, Lt. Albert Sidney Johnston wrote: "After marching 23 miles (from Turtle Village) this day, we camped by a small lake, and had to drink the water, which was very bad, but it was all that could be found. Here General Atkinson had, on this night, breastworks thrown up, which was easily done, as we encampled in thick timber...(July 2). This morning the army proceeded almost directly north towards Lake Coshkonong." Among Captain Early's mounted scouts was the 23-year-old Abraham Lincoln, finishing his third 30-day enlistment. General Atkinson's Army of the Frontier had entered Wisconsin at Turtle Village (Beloit) where it camped on June 30. It then moved north through the Priarie Road area to this lake-east of Milton. On July 2, the army moved north again and camped on Otter Creek about two miles east of Lake Koshkonong, before entering Jefferson County. At Cold Spring, on July 10, Lincoln was mustered out, his horse was stolen, and he returned by foot and canoe to New Salem, Illinois. 1976. [42.776664, -88.936424]

26. FORT KOSHKONONG. "Whilst lying here we have thrown up a stockade work flanked by four block houses for the security of our supplies and the accommodation of the sick," wrote General Henry Atkinson of this spot in his report to General Winfield Scott on July 17, 1832. Atkinson with more than 4,000 frontier soldiers had followed Black Hawk and his British Band up the Rock River in an attempt to end the Black Hawk War. After an unproductive sortie east up Bark River, Atkinson returned and built Fort Koshkonong later known as Fort Atkinson. The fort, constructed of oak logs eight feet tall, was abandoned when the army pursued and defeated Black Hawk at the Battle of Bad Axe in August 1832. Thus ended the Sauk's last hard fight against continued encroachment of white men onto their tribal lands. In September of 1836, Dwight Foster arrived and erected the first cabin in what is now Fort Atkinson. He and other settlers used logs from the stockade to build cabins, river rafts and for firewood. By 1840 little of the fort remained. Erected 1966 Fort Atkinson Historical Society. [42.92676, -88.831493]

27. BATTLE OF HORSESHOE BEND. At this place on June 16, 1832 between Wisconsin pioneers, under Colonel Henry Dodge, and a band of Black Hawk's Sacs was fought The Battle of the Pecatonica. The Annals of Indian Warfare offer no parallel to this battle. Of the twenty-one volunteer soldiers engaged, three were mortally wounded and one severely wounded. The seventeen Indians were slain. Thus was our land made safe for settlement. Erected by the Rhoda Hinsdale Chapter Daughters of the American Revolution of Shullsburg and the Town of Wiota 1922. [42.659246, -89.879602]

28. BATTLE OF PECATONICA. Blackhawk Memorial Park is on the site of the Battle of Pecatonica, the first of three military engagements fought in present-day Wisconsin during the American-Indian conflict of 1832 known as the Black Hawk War. On June 16, 1832, following attacks on settlers and miners at Fort Blue Mounds and Spafford's farm near Wiota, Colonel Henry Dodge led a group of frontier militia across the open prairie to this site in pursuit of a band of Kickapoo followers of Chief Black Hawk. Crossing the deep stream, the Indians took a defensive position along the steep banks of an oxbow lake near a bend in the Pecatonica River. Dodge and twenty-nine mounted militiamen soon arrived, fording the river to the north. Dodge sent four men to observe movement from high points along the river (at the east side of the park); four stayed with the horses. The others moved

through swamps to some timber, getting within thirty yards before the Kickapoo reportedly commenced firing. At Dodge's command the militia charged and engaged in hand-to-hand combat. After only a few minutes, all seventeen Kickapoo perished. Three frontiersmen were mortally wounded, and one was slightly injured. Dodge's decisive victory at this brief skirmish boosted the morale among settlers in the Lead Mining Region and U.S. Soldiers in pursuit of Black Hawk's band of Sac, Fox, and Kickapoo. The war ended forty-seven days later following the Battles of Wisconsin Heights (Dane County) and Bad Axe on the Mississippi River (Vernon County). The end of the conflict opened southern Wisconsin to increased settlement by farmers and miners. The Pecatonica battlefield site was listed on the State and National Registers of Historic Places in 2011. [42.661749, -89.877233]

29. OLD LEAD ROAD. In 1828, Ox-Teams, guided along an ancient Winnebago Indian Trail, began hauling lead from Exeter to Mineral Point and Gelena over this road. June 29, 1832, after the battle of the Pecatonica, General Henry Dodge and his rangers passed here to join the main pursuit of Black Hawk at Koshkonong. June 27, 1845 Niklaus Durst and Fridolin Streiff were led by this road to the site of New Glarus which they selected as the location of their Swiss Colony. August 15, 1845, the first band of Swiss Colonists followed this road to their new home. [42.787106, -89.629817]

30. SITE OF BLUE MOUNDS FORT. Built in May 1832 by the miners and settlers of the neighborhood and garrisoned by them as volunteer members of General Henry Dodge's Iowa-Michigan brigade from May 20 to September 20, 1832 during the Black Hawk War. This site was donated to the State Historical Society of Wisconsin by the heirs of Colonel Ebenezer Brigham pioneer settler who helped build the fort. Dedicated September 5, 1921, by the State Historical Society of Wisconsin. [43.005514, -89.829589]

31. SITE OF FORT JACKSON. In June, 1832 an alarm spread throughout the mining region that Black Hawk and his band were on the march north from Illinois. Hastily built stockades were erected throughout the lead region. Fort Jackson was built on this site using vertically placed logs arranged in a square that enclose cabins housing the garrison and their families. Two-story blockhouses fitted with gun ports were installed on the south east and north west corners. Fort Jackson served mainly to distribute military supplies during the Black Hawk War and was dismantled shortly thereafter. Erected 2002. Wisconsin Historical Society. [42.858970, -90.177105]

32. BLUE MOUNDS FORT. The onset of the Black Hawk War in northwestern Illinois in April, 1832 triggered panic in southwestern Wisconsin's lead mining region, prompting erection of over a dozen stockades. On an open prairie knoll ¾ mile south of this marker, area miners and settlers who became part of Colonel Henry Dodge's militia built Blue Mounds Fort. Here the Hall sisters, survivors of the Indian Creek massacre, were released for ransom through Winnebago intercession. W.G. Aubrey, George Foce and Emerson Green died in ambush attacks near the stockade. After the Battle of Wisconsin Heights, troops regrouped here. Despite repeated surrender attempts, Black Hawk's band of Sac and Fox Indians was virtually annihilated at the junction of the Bad Axe and Mississippi Rivers August 2. Thus ended one Native American group's efforts to escape the tragic consequences of white settlement. The heirs of Ebenezer Brigham donated a portion of the Fort site to the State Historical Society in 1921. Erected by the Dane County Historical Society 1992. [43.01504, -89.826559]

33. SITE OF FORT JACKSON. In June 1832, an alarm spread throughout the mining region that Black Hawk and his band were on the march north from Illinois. Hastily build stockades were erected throughout the lead region. Fort Jackson was built on this site using vertically placed logs arranged in a square that enclosed cabins housing the garrison and their families. Two-story blockhouses fitted with gun ports were installed on the southeast and northwest corners. Fort Jackson served mainly to distribute supplies during the Black Hawk War and was dismantled shortly thereafter. [42.858967, -90.177233]

34. OCOOCH MOUNTAINS. During the Black Hawk War of 1832, Black Hawk's band and the pursing military ventured into this unknown terrain of steep ridges and valleys. Following nearby Mill Creek, some of the band headed over these rugged hills known as the Ocooch Mountains. Along the way, many Indians died from exhaustion, starvation and battle wounds. Erected 1998. [43.334266, -90.525948]

35. DODGE'S GROVE. Dodge's Grove and Fort Union. Arriving in Dodgeville in 1827, Henry Dodge, a later renowned Black Hawk War military leader, territorial governor and state senator, began his Wisconsin career as a miner. In circa 1830, Dodge established living quarters and a large two-furnace smelting and mining operation at this site, a few miles south of Dodgeville. Bringing his family, slaves and about 200 miners to work at

this location. Dodge constructed many log dwellings and a stockade, later known as Fort Union during the Black Hawk War. Erected 1998. [42.9163, -90.118067]

36. FORT DEFIANCE. Fort Defiance was one of the last garrisoned stockade forts constructed in Territorial Wisconsin. Located in the booming lead mining region, an area of early settlement, the fort was built by local settlers in 1832 when developing tensions over Indian land rights erupted in the Black Hawk War. Although Fort Defiance did not undergo attack, it did have a garrison of about forty militia men who were said to be among the best drilled in the territory. The fort stood on the hill about 300 yards east of here and was enclosed by a sharply pointed palisade of heavy timbers set face to face, creating an almost impenetrable wall except for the musket loop holes. Measuring eighty feet wide by 120 feet long and eighteen feet high. Fort Defiance had two block houses located at opposite corners of the stockade. Within the walls were two buildings used to accommodate the garrison and the families of settler in case of a siege. There are no visible remains left of Fort Defiance. Erected 1988. [42.796433, -90.12935]

37. THE TRAGEDY OF WAR. On July 21, 1832 during the Black Hawk War, the U.S. Militia "passed through the narrows of the four lakes," Madison's Isthmus, in pursuit of Sac Indian leader Black Hawk and his band. Near this location, the Militia shot and scalped an old Sac warrior awaiting his death upon his wife's freshly dug grave. Erected 1998. [43.075637, -89.376642]

38. TRAIL DISCOVERY. On July 18th, during the Black Hawk War of 1832, Little Thunder—a Ho-Chunk (Winnebago) Indian guide to the U.S. Militia— discovered Black Hawk's Band crossed the Rock River in this vicinity. After receiving the news, General James D. Henry and Colonel Henry Dodge and the militia also crossed the river and followed the band's trail west. Erected 1998. [43.194324, -88.724668]

39. THIRD LAKE PASSAGE. On July 20th, during the Black Hawk War of 1832, Black Hawk led about 700 Sac, Fox and Kickapoo Indians past this point and through the "Third Lake Passage" the juncture of the Yahara River and Lake Monona. By sunset the military also reached the passage but abandoned their chase at nightfall to camp in this vicinity. Erected 1998. [43.090476, -89.333958]

APPENDIX D

40. FOUR LAKES ISTHMUS. Black Hawk, Sauk Chief, retreated through these grounds July 21, 1832, pursued by militia and U.S. regulars. Placed by the class of 1888 U.W. June 17, 1913. [43.076075, -89.404608]

41. PHEASANT BRANCH ENCAMPMENT. On the night of July 20th, during the Black Hawk War of 1832, Sac Indian leader Black Hawk and his followers camped near this location. Desperate for food and freightened by the approaching military, the Indians fled northwest towards the Wisconsin River the next morning. Erected 1998. [43.122442, -89.491321]

42. THE PURSUIT WEST. During the Black Hawk War of 1832, Black Hawk and his band fled down the Wisconsin River after the July 21st Battle of Wisconsin Heights. Two miles west of here, where the Pine River flows into the Wisconsin, the band left the Wisconsin River and headed north up the Pine River Valley. Erected 1998. [43.395433, -90.774517]

43. BATTLE OF WISCONSIN HEIGHTS. On July 21, 1832, during a persistent rainstorm the 65-year old Sac Indian leader, Black Hawk led 60 of his Sac and Fox and Kickapoo warriors in a holding action against 700 United States militia at this location. The conflict, known as the Battle of Wisconsin Heights, was the turning point in the Black Hawk War. Here commanders General James D. Henry and Colonel Henry Dodge and their troops overtook Black Hawk and his followers after pursuing them for weeks over the marshy areas and rough terrain of south central Wisconsin. Yet because of Black Hawk's superb military strategy, the steady rain and nightfall, approximately 700 Indians, including childran and the aged, escaped down or across the Wisconsin River about one mile west of here. Their success was short-lived. The war ended just 12 days later at the Battle of Bad Axe when many of Black Hawk's followers drowned or were slain in their attempt to cross the Mississippi River. Erected 1998. [43.244576, -89.723365]

44. INDIAN LAKE PASSAGE. On July 21, 1832, during the Black Hawk War, Sac Indian leader Black Hawk and his band left Pheasant Branch, west of Madison, retreating ahead of the military forces commanded by Colonels Ewing and Dodge. The band fled north following a route past the west end of Indian Lake and turned westward down the broad valley now bisected by Highway 12. The military, despite rain and exhausted horses managed to catch up to Black Hawk's warriors late that afternoon at the Heights over

looking the Wisconsin River. Erected 1997 by the Dane County Historical Society. [43.189072, -89.634959]

45. BATTLE OF WISCONSIN HEIGHTS. Original Marker. Near this site the Sauk Chieftain Black Hawk and his band were overtaken by Wisconsin and Illinois troops on July 21, 1832. Erected by the John Bell Chapter of DAR Madison, September 3, 1923. [43.244939, -89.723178]

46. SITE OF OLD HELENA. A thriving and important town of Lead-Mining days. Here on July 28, 1832 troops crossed the Wisconsin River in pursuit of Indians under Black Hawk. Among officers of the army here present these later became distinguished. Gen. Henry Atkinson, Col. Zachary Taylor, Col. Nathan Boone, Capt. William S. Harney, Col. Hugh Brady, Lt. Robert Anderson, Col. Henry Dodge, Lt. Jefferson Davis, Lt. Albert Sidney Johnston. State Historical Society of Wisconsin. 1925. [43.147772, -90.046828]

47. TROOP ENCAMPMENT. According to local tradition, on the night of July 29, 1832, during the Black Hawk War, General Atkinson's troops camped at this location. The next day, the troops proceeded up the West Branch of the Pine River, only to abandon their supply wagon in this rough terrain. Erected 1988. [43.445342, -90.362567]

48. MILITARY RIVER CROSSING. In this vicinity, during the Black Hawk War of 1832, General Henry Atkinson and approximately 1,000 soldiers crossed the Wisconsin River in pursuit of Sac Indian leader Black Hawk and his followers. On July 26th at the old abandoned Village of Helena, the soldiers dismantled the village's buildings to make rafts for the crossing. Erected 1998. [43.143322, -90.06037]

49. BLACK HAWK TRAIL—CV PORTER 1. 700 Sac Indians July 31. 1200 Soldiers August 1, 1832. Followed this ridge west into Vernon County over this ground. Two human skeletons were found at a spring west of Wilder's Hotel, Rising Sun in 1852. Nancy Wilber authority 1892. [CV Porter]. [43.418166, -90.958506]

50. ATKINSON ENCAMPMENT—CV PORTER 2. On night of August 1 and 2 1832, Gen. Atkinson's army of 1,200 mounted men in pursuit of Black Hawk encamped on this area from 8 p.m. to 3 a.m. CV Porter 2. [43.459874, -91.06236]

51. BLACK HAWK ENCAMPMENT—CV PORTER 3. At shallow pond 115 rods due south Blackhawk's 700 Sac Indians encamped July 31 1832. Soldiers found six decrepit Indians here and "left them behind."...Lee Sterling in 1846 found a handful of silver brooches here. CV Porter 3. [43.459874, -91.06236]

52. BLACK HAWK AND WINNEBAGO TRAIL—CV PORTER 4. Black Hawk and Winnebago Trail. Two trails ran across Dr. Bean's door yard, the Black Hawk retreat and the Winnebago Trail which ran from Winneshieks (De Soto) village to large Winnebago town above the forks of the Kickapoo at Manning prior to 1840. Authority Dr. D.A. Bean 1854. Wm. T. Sterling 1840. CV Porter 4. [43.466169, -91.09609]

53. BLACK HAWK OUTPOST—CV PORTER 5. August 2, 1832. Twenty picked Sacs were stationed here to decoy the US Army northward and permit the Indian main body with women and children to escape across the river fourteen of the outpost were shot here while trying to surrender. In 1846 LeGrand Sterling found twelve human skeletons near here. No 5. CVP 1930 S. [43.470671, -91.17013]

54. BATTLE BLUFF—CV PORTER 6. Elv 1139FT. Battle Hollow. Severe fighting one mile east between Gen. Henry's 300 Ill. Militia and 300 Sac Indians Aug. 2 1832. Battle Island. Hard fighting opposite. 1200 white soldiers engaged. 17 killed. 12 wounded of Indians. 150 shot. 150 drowned, 50 taken prisoners. 300 crossed river of whom 150 were killed by Sioux instigated by Gen. Atkinson. Of the 1,000 Sacs who crossed the river from Iowa in April 1832, "not more than 150 survived to tell the tragic story of the Black Hawk War." R.G. Thwaites. CV Porter. [43.456836, -91.213277]

55. SOLDIERS GROVE ORIGIN. In late July, 1832, during the Black Hawk War, Sac Indian leader Black Hawk led his starving followers through this area in their escape from the General Henry Atkinson and his military forces. After Black Hawk's brilliant delaying tactics at the Battle of Wisconsin Heights, he fled with his band towards the Mississippi River. On August 1st, in their pursuit of Black Hawk, about 1,300 United States army and militia, including notable future leaders, Col. Zachary Taylor, Col. Henry Dodge, and Albert Sidney Johnson, encamped in this vicinity, known then as Pine Village. Weary from their trek through the rugged terrain, foraged in the grass here. Because this military encampment became widely known

throughout the territory, Pine Grove Village was renamed Soldiers Grove. Erected 1998. [43.395901, -90.774731].

56. HEAD OF BATTLE ISLE. On the eve of Aug 1, 1832, Black Hawk and his men with a flag of truce, went to the head of this island to surrender to the Captain of the steamer "Warrior." Whites on boat asked are you Winnebagoes or Sacs. Sacs, replied Black Hawk. A load of canister was at once fired, killing 28 Indians suing for peace. Major Zebulon M. Pike encamped on this island on Sept 9th 1905. Here lived Nora Spaulding who in Oct 1904 rode an unbroken colt to Victory at 2 a.m. and saved a limited train from going thru a burned culvert. CV Porter 6. [43.455143, -91.22621]

57. BATTLE OF BAD AXE. After holding off his pursuers at the Battle of Wisconsin Heights (about 1½ miles south of present Sauk City) Black Hawk led his people over unfamiliar country toward the Mississippi. In the meantime, the Army alerted Fort Crawford at Prairie du Chien. When the Indians reached the Mississippi, they found an armed steamboat blocking escape. The Battle of Bad Axe fought near here August 1–2, 1832 ended the Black Hawk War. Driven into the water by their pursuers, the Indians—warriors, old people, women and children—were shot down or drowned as they tried to escape. Black Hawk succeeded in getting away but was soon taken prisoner. Later, when asked about his ill-fated venture, he said simply: "Rock River was a beautiful country; I love my towns, my cornfields and the home of my people. I fought for it." [43.456919, -91.213217]

58. BLACK HAWK'S SURRENDER. On August 2, 1832, the Black Hawk War effectively ended when the U.S. Military massacred many followers of the Sauk Indian leader Black Hawk at the Battle of Bad Axe, located about 35 miles north of here. Black Hawk, known as Ma-ka-tai-me-she-kia-kiak, his advisor The Prophet and some of his followers, escaped north to a Ho-Chunk (Winnebago) village near Prairie La Crosse. There, One-Eyed Decorah, Chasja-ka, and other Ho-Chunk persuaded the fugitives to surrender to the American authorities. They journeyed down the Mississippi River to Prairie du Chien where Black Hawk and The Prophet were delivered to U.S. Indian Agent, Gen. Joseph Street. Attired in resplendent white deerskin clothing provided by the Ho-Chunk, Black Hawk formally surrendered to Gen. Street on August 27, 1832, and was briefly imprisoned at Fort Crawford under the command of Col. Zachary

Taylor. Lt. Jefferson Davis was charged with transporting Black Hawk to Jefferson Barracks in St. Louis and Black Hawk was imprisoned there until the following spring when President Andrew Jackson ordered his release. Erected 1999. [43.0426, -91.147092]

59. JEFFERSON DAVIS. 1808–1889. Lieutenant United States Army. Assigned to Fort Crawford 1831 served here with distinction during Black Hawk War. Hero in Mexican War 1846–1848. United States Congressman, Senator, Secretary of War, President Confederate States of America 1861–1865. Erected by the United Daughters of the Confederacy. [43.047102, -91.146436]

60. DECORAH PEAK. The rock-crested hill to the east was named after One-Eyed Decorah, a Winnebago Chief who, according to tradition, took refuge in a cave near the peak after being wounded in a Chippewa attack on his village. He remained in hiding throughout the bloody engagement and then at nightfall made his way down the Black River to another Winnebago settlement. The next day he returned, surprised the celebrating Chippewa and routing them. With other Wisconsin Chief, he signed a treaty with the United States at Prairie du Chien on August 19, 1825, establishing tribal boundaries in the hope of sercuring a "firm and perpetual peace." He achieved his greatest renown after the Black Hawk War when he accompanied the defeated Black Hawk and the Prophet to Prairie du Chien, where on August 27, 1832, the two Sauk leaders surrendered. Erected 1958. [44.071066, -91.321584]

61. SOP-HO-KAB. Sop-Ho-Kab was a seven-year-old full-blooded Sauk Indian and survivor of the Battle of Bad Axe (i.e., Bad Axe Massacre), which took place on August 2, 1832, near Victory, Wisconsin. For several painful days after the battle she floated down the Mississippi River in a canoe with a severely wounded Sauk brave. Arriving at Olde Jordan's Landing (later Dunleith, Illinois) tired, scared, starving, lonely, and exhausted, she was found, adopted, and raised by Thomas and Mary (Whiteside) Jordan, owners of Jordan's Ferry. Thomas Jordan died suddenly in 1833 and Mary Jordan raised "Indian Kate" with their fourteen children. Catherine Clare Jordan grew and married Probus Eberle, son of Sales and Antonious (Kist) Eberle, a prominent Prussian immigrant farmer. They raised their eight children on a farm a couple of miles from the Mississippi River in section 21, Jo Daviess County. Probus died in 1890 and Catherine sold their farm a few

years later. She then resided in Wiota, Cass County, Iowa, and Centralia, today west of Dubuque, Iowa, with her son John Bunyon Eberle. She then moved to Cassville, Wisconsin, to stay with Fred and Catherine Clare (her daughter) Fishnick where she died on November 9, 1899. She is buried with her husband, Probus, in the East Dubuque Cemetery in Plots 1 & 2, one mile from the library up Hill Street. Dedicated August 2017, during the 185th anniversary of Thomas Jordan's rescue of Sop-Ho-Kab, whom he affectionately called "Katie." [42.4922, -90.6424]

62. EMIGRANT INDIANS IN KANSAS. As the nation pushed west, Indian Tribes were removed from their lands. Between 1825 and 1850, 25 tribes were relocated to Kansas. Two tiny strips of land in extreme northeast Kansas were set aside for the Iowa and the Sac and Fox. Relocation meant learning to survive with different natural resources. [39.862389, -95.227687]

63. WINNEBAGO INDIANS. Winnebago Indians call themselves "Hochunkgra." A Siouan people, they once occupied the southern half of Wisconsin and the northern counties of Illinois. The Black Hawk War of 1832 and a series of treaties forced the Winnebago out of their homeland, and they were removed to reservations in Iowa, Minnesota, South Dakota and finally a portion of the Omaha Reservation in Nebraska. With each removal, small bands of Winnebago returned to Wisconsin, with the largest settlement in Jackson County. About seven miles east of Black River Falls is the historic Winnebago Indian Mission, founded by the German Reformed Church in 1878. The Mission includes about half of the Winnebago population of Jackson County, the powwow grounds, Indian Cemetery and Mitchell Red Cloud Memorial. Tribal traditions are preserved through the clan system, the Medicine Lodge, and War Bundle Fest. Erected 1974. [44.228009, -90.708328]

RESOURCES AND FURTHER READING

Black Hawk's Autobiography: Autobiography of Ma-ka-tai-me-she-kia-kiak, or Black Hawk. Available via Hathitrust.com or GoogleBooks.com.

Cherokee Phoenix and Indians' Advocate. This newspaper was launched in 1828 in Georgia. It provided an outlet for Native Americans to share their own opinions and stories to English-language readers. The newspaper printed articles side by side in English and Cherokee. While the views aren't that of the Sac and Fox, the paper did report on the Black Hawk War conflict. The paper provided a unique voice in early American discourse, as the editor described its mission as hoping to "diffuse knowledge among the Cherokees, as well as in making their grievances be known abroad." The Library of Congress is working with state and private libraries to undertake the herculean task of digitizing and publishing America's newspapers online. While this laudable endeavor will take years if not decades to complete, more than 1.5 million pages from regional and local newspapers are already posted. The project's goal is to continue to make accessible to the public digital archival American newspapers from 1789 to 1963. chroniclingamerica.loc.gov.

Sangamon Journal. The frontier newspaper from Abraham Lincoln's pioneer region has been digitized and made freely available online by the Illinois Digital Newspaper Collections through a project of the library at the University of Illinois. The collection includes Lincoln's first letter announcing his candidacy in 1832. idnc.library.illinois.edu.

Smithsonian American Art Museum. In 2020, the digital art archives of the SAAM released 2.8 million images into an open-access online platform for the public. The images in this book from the SAAM archives represent a small sampling of the historical material curated by the SAAM. americanart. si.edu.

INDEX

INDEX

ABOUT THE AUTHOR

B en Strand hails from the Uplands of southwestern Wisconsin. He received his education while serving as a busboy at the Thym's Supper Club in Dodgeville, Wisconsin, and the Old Mexico Grill in Santa Fe, New Mexico. With degrees from the University of Wisconsin and an MFA from Goddard College in Vermont, he has a long-standing commitment to the Wisconsin Idea and the Green Mountain Ideal. As a lifelong Cubs fan, he smartly swore off the lovable losers when they removed the communal urinals from Wrigley Field, which just happened to be the year before they ruined a perfectly honorable losing streak. He currently makes his home with his family and school-age children in the Driftless region of Wisconsin. After many years of avid prickly ash pruning, he has forged a truce with this native bush and is now focused on removing the twenty-first-century scourge of burdock, wild parsnips and multiflora rose. Invitations and admonitions can be directed to ben@benstrand.com.

Visit us at
www.historypress.com